THE MEASUREMENT OF UTILITY

THE MEASUREMENT
OF UTILITY

BY

TAPAS MAJUMDAR

LONDON
MACMILLAN & CO LTD
NEW YORK · ST MARTIN'S PRESS
1966

MACMILLAN AND COMPANY LIMITED
Little Essex Street London WC 2
also Bombay Calcutta Madras Melbourne

THE MACMILLAN COMPANY OF CANADA LIMITED
70 Bond Street Toronto 2

ST MARTIN'S PRESS INC
175 Fifth Avenue New York NY 10010

PRINTED IN GREAT BRITAIN

Preface

The following study was first undertaken as a collection of essays at the London School of Economics during October 1955 to June 1957 under the supervision of Lionel Robbins and (excepting for the first and the last terms) Dr. George Morton. Impossible as it is to express the author's indebtedness to his supervisors with any adequacy at all, he wishes particularly to mention that had it not been for Professor Robbins, he would never have seen that the collection of essays could (as it eventually did) achieve the unity of a single thesis. And had it not been for George Morton, many more stylistic blemishes would have remained undetected.

The author has tried, as far as possible, to specify the extent of his indebtedness to particular contributors in the body of the text. Needless to add, it is beyond his powers to recognise fully all the different sources from which his ideas have originated. The influence of other authors would, in any case, be often quite apparent to the reader. What would not be apparent, however, except to those few who, like the present author, have passed through the hands of Panchanan Chakrabartty and Bhabatosh Datta at the University of Calcutta, is how much the present study owes directly or indirectly to their teachings. The memory of Professor Datta's literary exposition of the most difficult reaches of welfare economics has, in particular, always been a source of inspiration to the present author.

Finally, the author wishes to record his sense of gratitude to his friend Dipak Banerjee, whose enthusiasm for the present study and erudition in methodology had made him for the author, at all hours of the day (and night) a ready source of reference. To Dr. Satyesh Chakrabartty the author is indebted for much expert help in removing some of the clumsiness from the few diagrams which occur in the following pages.

The author is also glad to acknowledge the generosity of the Government of India whose award of an overseas scholarship made his visit to England possible, and of the authorities of the Presidency College, Calcutta, in granting the necessary leave of absence.

In deference to an old Indian custom the author must forbear from trying to express his gratitude to his mother, without whose vigilant insistence the present work would never have been completed in time.

T. M.

Contents

Foreword

The pure theory of value is not one of those branches of economic analysis which have any immediate bearing on practice. No politician will alter his line of policy, no business executive will change his programme, because of some improvement in the presentation of preference systems or in the definition of indifference in choice. Yet, like the pure theory of numbers in mathematics, it has had a perennial fascination for some of the best minds in our subject; and experience suggests that excellence here is a hallmark of high competence in theoretical economics generally. It is surely no accident that so many of the leaders of the profession to-day, the Allens, the Hicks, the Samuelsons, have graduated, so to speak, in this specialism. But at the same time it is a subject of exceptional intellectual difficulty and a subject in which failure is all too easy.

In choosing, therefore, as a young teacher on leave from a great Indian university, to spend the all too short time available to him in work in this exacting field rather than on a theme with a more immediate and practical appeal, Dr. Majumdar has shown great courage and great devotion to the pursuit of abstract truth. The result, I think, has fully justified his choice. The problem of the mode and manner in which what economists call utility can (or cannot) be conceived to be measured, which has been the special subject of his research, has been one of the most extensively discussed questions of pure theory in recent years; and, if only as a guide to the history of thought, a systematic survey was a real *desideratum*. In fact, in my judgment, Dr. Majumdar has provided considerably more than this. With his clear and orderly weighing of the different points of view and with his modest but well-argued constructions, it seems to me that he has made a distinct and significant contribution of his own. In this I may be biased; for, whatever reserves I may have on minor matters, I confess I find his main position, midway between the extremes of flatfooted cardinalism at one end and radical behaviourism at the other, one which is highly congenial and convincing. But I hope that, whether or not his final conclusions be found acceptable, it will be generally agreed that the process of exposition and discussion which leads up to them is in itself thoroughly worth while and constitutes a valuable addition to the literature of the debate.

In his preface Dr. Majumdar pays a very kind but very undeserved tribute to my part as his supervisor. It is because, in that capacity, I learnt so much more from him than I was able to give in return, that I venture to believe that others, sharing an interest in the subject, will find pleasure and stimulus in his lucid and penetrating analysis.

LIONEL ROBBINS

LONDON SCHOOL OF ECONOMICS
7th November, 1957

Introduction

The present study is designed to be mainly a methodological contribution to utility (economic welfare) theory. It is not a study in welfare economics.

In the following pages we have inquired into the meaning and (operational) consequences of the concept of measurable utility in economics. Our study, quite justifiably therefore, has been based on an appraisal of the measurability controversy in utility theory which has (explicitly or implicitly) been going on in the literature for (at least) the last twenty-five years.[1]

We have found it convenient to divide the following chapters into two parts. Part I is devoted mainly to definitions, and Part II to propositions regarding the nature and significance of utility which have generally been advanced in theoretical welfare economics.

Conclusions as to the measurability of welfare or utility rest, in the final analysis, on the resolution of a set of distinct, irreducible, unavoidable questions. It will be our purpose in Part I to lay down these questions and to draw out their distinctions at some length. It is only by the end of Part II that it would be fully apparent how easily and how often faulty end-results have cropped up in welfare economics when some of these questions were either confused or illegitimately bypassed.

[1] The present controversy, perhaps, can be said to have been touched off by Hicks and Allen in 'A Reconsideration of the Theory of Value', *Economica*, 1934.

The very first question that arises is naturally that of the meaning of utility or welfare.[1] It will be seen that this question has been made further complicated in the literature of welfare economics by the introduction of the notion of 'economic' welfare, as distinct from other forms of welfare. In Chapter I, we shall argue that the dichotomy between economic and non-economic forms of welfare is meaningless, and that the conventional Pigovian use of the term 'economic welfare'— and that, of course, is also its literal use — is quite insupportable except when referring to the imaginary world of the classical 'Economic Man'. It will be our conclusion however, that there may nevertheless be a certain justification for retaining the attribute 'economic' while referring to welfare in the discussion of economic policy, if only to emphasise the point that only those aspects of individual or social welfare which are capable of being stated as ends of consciously husbanded effort, are to be the subject-matter of welfare economics.

Having disposed of the Pigovian complication in the theory of welfare referred to above, we shall proceed to the question of the meaningfulness of welfare perception in the second chapter. At this stage however, we shall find it necessary to introduce an axiom, which would henceforth be implicit throughout the rest of our analysis.

Simply stated, the axiom will be that the welfare of any individual is perceived, in the first place, by the same individual. This seemingly innocent axiom, it may be ob-

[1] 'Welfare' and 'Utility' have been used in identical sense throughout the rest of the study, a simplification which would not probably commend itself to the neo-cardinalist behaviourists. Cf. A. A. Alchian, 'The Meaning of Utility Measurement', *American Economic Review*, 1953. Both terms, however, can and have been used in a purely non-normative sense.

served, does not, however, command a certain acceptance. In fact, a dominant section of contemporary political and social philosophy appears to be built specifically upon its denial. There will therefore be, a primary bias, which we wish to make quite explicit, in our statement of the theory of welfare perception. But it is only fair to add that though our axiom links the concept of welfare inalienably to the individual, it seems to us that none of the usual ideals of socialism need be in logical conflict with it.

Having discussed the definition of welfare and the meaning of welfare perception we shall now be in a position to raise the crucial question: that of welfare measurability. Our object in Chapter III is to establish and emphasise the logical distinction between *absolute* identifiability and the measurability of welfare.[1] We shall demonstrate that while the cardinal hypothesis *requires* absolute identifiability of welfare, the ordinalist case would be the same whether welfare is assumed to be absolutely or only relatively discernible.

In Part II (as would also be evident from the table of contents), we have found it useful to distinguish between utility theories not only (*a*) on the basis of whether the cardinalist or the ordinalist hypothesis is admitted, but also (*b*) on the basis of whether the definition of utility is made in behaviourist (choice) or introspectionist (preference) terms. We shall find that each of the four possible combinations of (*a*) and (*b*) will have the characteristics of its own brand of utility theory methodologically given.

[1] Absolute identification without at least ordinal measurability (e.g., perception of good or bad *without* perceptions of better or worse) has, of course, no meaning in economics, and must be ruled out of an *operational* definition of utility.

In course of our comparative study of the four types of utility theory we have tried to demonstrate the relative advantages of the Hicksian[1] indifference-preference (ordinalist-introspective) hypothesis *both on operational and on other grounds:* which, therefore, provides our principal thesis.

Chapter IV (which is the opening chapter of Part II), contains a brief exposition of the method of testing the different utility theories which has been used by us. Chapters V to IX cover the theories of Marshall (introspective-cardinalist), Hicks (introspective-ordinalist), Samuelson (behaviourist-ordinalist), Morgenstern and Neumann and their followers (behaviourist-cardinalist) and Armstrong (introspective-cardinal-revivalist) respectively. The Tenth and concluding chapter is devoted to a final summing up of the measurability problem in utility theory.

[1] We part ways with Hicks on so many vital points that we may best confess here what must soon be obvious: that we have used 'Hicksian' only in an 'ideal' sense, and that the ideal is ours.

PART I

DEFINITIONS

CHAPTER I

The Meaning and Scope of Economic Welfare

I

In many senses the origin of welfare economics as a distinct body of doctrines has been the result of a reaction: it has existed mainly to refute the abstract world of the classical Economic Man. The Economic Man is truly the knight of popular mythology. His is the solitary figure of the Subject facing the Object, which is the rest of the universe. In this Subject-Object relationship the Economic Man has no collaborator and no human opponent. But the central figure of classical economics need not be regarded as a particularly romantic personality. It goes without saying that he is assumed to be absolutely and narrowly self-centred.[1] What requires further emphasising is that his motives are constructed to be purely *monetary*. From which two attributes of the Economic Man would clearly stand out. In the first place, he is unaffected by (and incapable of affecting) what happened to others. In the second place, he would not pursue a target which could not directly or indirectly be brought into relationship with the measuring

[1] An underlying welfare assumption was, of course, present. It was simply that 'by pursuing his own interest he (every individual) frequently promotes that of the society more effectually than when he really intends to promote it'. (Adam Smith in *Wealth of Nations*, Modern Library Edition, p. 423.)

rod of money. The first attribute postulates the absence of external economies; the second defines the end of economic activity solely in terms of marketable output. Welfare economics in the hands of Professor Pigou was the refutation of the first attribute of the Economic Man: it was an elaboration of the external economies argument.[1] The distinction between the marginal social and the marginal private products of individual effort was the corner-stone of Pigovian welfare economics.

In quite an important sense, however, the Pigovian welfare economics failed to tear itself away completely from the notion of the Economic Man. This was mainly due to its implicit acceptance of the second attribute of the Subject: that he must not be presumed to have tangible ends other than those which could somehow be translated into marketable slices of the Gross National Product. In the curious world of the *homo oeconomicus* all social activities conveniently and simply arrange themselves into two categories: those which are economic, and those which are not. The welfare of the individual, which is the result of these activities, is therefore made up of two easily distinguished parts: that which is economic and that which is not. And, of course, the test of admissibility of a particular type of activity as 'economic', is whether it could be described in terms of units of money. Economic welfare is thus very understandably defined by Professor Pigou as 'that part of general welfare which can be brought

[1] It may be remarked incidentally that the final extension of the external-economies argument consists in allowing for situations involving the use of strategy of a game-theory type. For a note on the possible use of the Theory of Games in ordinal utility theory, see Appendix (published as 'Choice and Revealed Preference', in *Econometrica*, January 1956).

directly or indirectly into relation with the measuring rod of money'.[1]

We do not need to repeat the formidable and now familiar set of arguments against the acceptability of money as the 'measuring rod', to be convinced of the inadequacy of the simple Pigovian definition of economic welfare. For one thing, the classical exponents of the measuring-rod thesis were themselves sufficiently aware of some of the limitations of the usefulness of money as a unit of measurement of welfare. It would perhaps save us a good deal of argument to have the testimony of the premier member of the classical 'Cardinal Club' on this point:

'Economics is, or aims at being, a science, concerned like other sciences with the organisation of knowledge of facts. Its ultimate subject-matter is economic welfare, also called satisfaction, a thing which "can be brought under the category of greater or less". In certain restricted situations we can measure satisfaction pretty well in terms of money: but on a larger canvas our measuring rod breaks down, and we have to be content to treat the stream of aggregate real income as an "objective counterpart" or indicator of the positive elements of economic welfare.'[2]

As we shall argue below, even this entirely apologetic version of the Pigovian definition of economic welfare is contestable at least on three grounds.

[1] A. C. Pigou, *The Economics of Welfare*, Second Edition.
[2] Sir Dennis H. Robertson, *Utility and All That and Other Essays*, Allen & Unwin, London, 1952, p. 14.
Note also the curious use of 'the positive elements of economic welfare'. What other elements can Sir Dennis have in mind?

II

The first and probably the most obvious objection would come from those who would regard the description of satisfaction as 'a thing which can be brought under the category of greater or less' as at least premature if not definitely misleading. The following hypothetical case would perhaps bring into relief the main point of this important objection.

Let us suppose that an individual is faced with two alternative welfare situations (however defined), X and Y. X may be as commonplace as the consumption of a cup of coffee, and Y the purchase of a copy of *The Times*, or either may be as complicated as a composite set of probabilities. It would perhaps be quite permissible to assume that the individual finds his welfare to be greater or less according as he gets more or less of X, other things remaining the same (provided of course that X constitutes a source of satisfaction). Similarly, it may be assumed that he finds his welfare position improves or deteriorates according as he has more or less of Y. In other words, it may perhaps justifiably be assumed that the individual's welfare, in so far as it related exclusively to X, or alternatively, to Y, is 'a thing which could be brought under the category of greater or less'. But that, unfortunately, is about as far as we can go without making a fresh assumption regarding the nature of welfare. We cannot, for example, take it for granted from the above that the individual could or would state a relation of preference (or indifference) *between* X and Y. It is conceivable that all that the individual would be able to say is that his enjoyment of X is *different* from his enjoyment of Y, and that therefore the two kinds of enjoyment were just not comparable. In such circumstances it would be hardly right to describe the individual's welfare as 'a thing', much less to claim that it could be brought under the category of greater or less. Unless the individual's world was known to consist of X or things like X and nothing else to choose from, or similarly, of Y and things like Y it cannot be taken for *granted* that for him welfare 'could be brought under the category of greater or less'.

Quite often, a movement from one situation to another may only imply for the individual concerned a change in the *character* of his enjoyment: so that as a result of the movement his welfare neither increases nor decreases nor yet remains the same! This does not mean, however, that when an individual is faced with two alternative welfare situations which he is unable to compare, he will choose neither. Unless of course, he wishes to make a famous ass of himself, he will take the one or the other rather than go without both. Faced with two non-comparable situations (or situations between which the individual is indifferent), he may follow any arbitrary criterion or none to make a choice. If he follows the same arbitrary criterion always, he would appear to be a consistent chooser; if he does not, he would appear to be inconsistent. If the former, he would be like the old lady who went to the races and *always* backed the horse with the longest name and was rightly renowned for her consistency. If the latter, he would be like the other old lady who also went to the races, but who chose her horse sometimes on the length of its tail and sometimes on the colour of its coat and was therefore known as particularly whimsical! It should be remarked that whichever course the individual may take, his choice would not reveal his (absence of) preference![1]

We must bear in mind, however, that to say that the assumption of comparability lies hidden in the Pigovian definition of welfare is not to say that we can do much better than that. All we can do is to recognise explicitly the situations and circumstances in which welfare economics must draw a blank not because of ignorance, but because of precise knowledge (that comparability does not exist)! We have argued later that when welfare is absolutely identifiable but not even ordinally measurable (two non-comparable welfare situations would provide just such an instance), we cannot include it in an operationally significant definition. But when we exclude such situations (and there we can be no better than the Pigovian), we must add a little rider, which is also a confession: that when such situations do come our way, we do not know what to do about them.

III

The second objection that can be made to the definition is that it is quite impossible to treat the stream of aggregate real income as the indicator of the 'positive elements of economic welfare' without assuming away the problem of the distribution of that income. Not only is it illegitimate to assume that the same stream of real income will imply the same level of welfare in whichever way people might

[1] The possibility of non-comparability provides another reason (apart from the possibilities of indifference and the deliberate use of deceptive stratagems) which should make us wary of the Revealed Preference Axiom!

be sharing it, an analysis of the index-number problem would show that such a statement as 'a larger (or smaller) real income' is implicitly biased in one direction or other if the *composition* of real income is not the same in the two compared situations. The following simplified two-person model would perhaps help demonstrate the importance of the 'index-number objection'.

Let us consider a community of two individuals A and B. Let us suppose, for the sake of simplicity that only two commodities, X and Y are available to A and B, which therefore are the only two constituents of the community's real national income. If the community were faced simply with the choice between two situations, one of which provided more of both X and Y than did the other, then obviously the *physical* size of the real national income could be said to be larger in one situation than in the other. Thus, for example, a real income of $5X$, $7Y$ could be said to be larger than one of $2X$, $5Y$. Whether this also implies that the welfare of the community is higher as it moves from $2X$, $5Y$ to $5X$, $7Y$ will, of course, depend on the additional consideration whether the change if any, in the relative shares of the real national income between A and B as a result of the movement, is to be regarded as desirable.

But a change even in the physical size of the national income would not quite be measurable if one of the constituents of income rises while another falls. Thus the two real-income situations $5X$, $7Y$ and $7X$, $5Y$ for example, would not be physically comparable. When we remember that many of the real-income changes over time for a community are likely to be of this type, we can realise how difficult it is to 'be content to treat the stream of aggregate real income as an "objective counterpart" or indicator of the positive elements of economic welfare'.

We may decide, however, to try to compare the two situations $5X$, $7Y$ and $7X$, $5Y$ by inviting the two members of the community to name these in the order of their preferences. The valuation of the real national income by each individual in that case should depend on two kinds of consideration. In the first place, the individual concerned would obviously be guided by his own relative preference of the two baskets of goods, assuming that he does not share his basket with the other person. In the second place, he would also consider his own expected share in the basket in either situation. His actual ordering would no doubt depend both on his tastes *and* his expected share in the distribution. It is possible, for example, that guided only by his relative preference of X and Y, the individual would prefer one particular basket which nevertheless he would reject if he is offered too small a share in it. Thus if the individual A prefers, say, $5X$, $7Y$ to $7X$, $5Y$ on the assumption that he has the whole of it, and similarly B prefers $7X$, $5Y$ to $5X$, $7Y$, it is still possible that given certain distributions of the two sets of real income between A and B, *both* may prefer one set to the other. In such a situation it is probably wise to say that the real national income is *higher* in one case than in the other. This interesting possibility may best be demonstrated diagrammatically following the technique adpoted in the construction of Samuelson's 'utility-possibility' curves.

In the diagram the ordering of the real national income by A is plotted along the W_A axis, so that points farther to the right represent relatively preferred situations.

Similarly the ordering by B is plotted along W_B. M_1N_1 represents all the possible distributions of $5X$, $7Y$ between A and B, which satisfy Pareto-optimum conditions,[1] so that the ascending order of A's preference is the descending

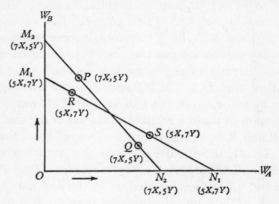

Diagram 1
Welfare Valuation of Real Income

order for B.[2] Similarly M_2N_2 represents the optimum distribution possibility of $7X$, $5Y$.

M_1 represents the situation in which B gets the whole of $5X$, $7Y$ and A gets nothing. At N_1, A gets everything and B gets nothing. As we move along the M_1N_1 line to the right we obtain better and better distribution situations for A and therefore worse and worse (since the optimum con-

[1] The Samuelsonian construction, it may be remarked, is an iso-resources-utility-possibility locus while ours is an iso-product-utility-possibility locus. Both require the fulfilment of Pareto-optimum conditions, so that there can be no distribution situation at which both A and B would be better off than at any point on the utility-possibility line.

[2] Note that the utility-possibility lines are ordinal; no restriction on them is stipulated except that they fall to the right.

ditions are satisfied) for B. Similarly for the real income $7X, 5Y$, M_2 represents the best situation for B and the worst for A; N_2 represents the best situation for A and the worst for B. Since guided by taste alone, A would prefer $5X, 7Y$ to $7X, 5Y$, N_1 appears to the right of N_2. Similarly since B would prefer $7X, 5Y$ to $5X, 7Y$, M_2 lies above M_1. The M_1N_1 and M_2N_2 lines, therefore, intersect each other.

We may now choose two distribution possibilities each of the two 'streams of aggregate real income' $5X, 7Y$ and $7X, 5Y$: P and Q on M_2N_2, and R and S on M_1N_1. A glance at the diagram will show that if A and B were called upon to make a relative valuation of the two situations P and R, both will place the former higher than the latter. Thus both will virtually have agreed that given one particular distribution of $7X, 5Y$ represented by P, and another of $5X, 7Y$ represented by R, the real national income $7X, 5Y$ is to be valued higher than the real national income $5X, 7Y$. If, however, we consider the two possibilities S and Q, we shall find that both the individuals find themselves at a higher level of welfare in the situation represented by S than in the one represented by Q. In other words, both A and B will value $5X, 7Y$ *above* $7X, 5Y$ this time, given the particular distributions.

These results would appear to be mutually contradictory only if the importance of the question of distribution in the evaluation of the national income is not sufficiently realised. It is, however, no more than simple common sense to suggest that the welfare content of income would be determined by the individual by the extent of his participation in it. So long as the notion of the community's income is sought to be derived in terms of individual welfare, the question of the valuation of that income cannot be distinguished from and is necessarily bound up in principle with the question of its distribution.

IV

Let us now turn to the third objection which the Pigovian definition of economic welfare would be open to. Briefly, it rests on the argument that it is improper to define economic welfare so narrowly as to identify its pursuit solely with the consumption and production of the National Product. In fact, the hitherto usual preoccupation with what has been produced (with or without consideration for how it has been distributed), and the consequent reluctance to regard any line of activity directed to non-output ends within the universe of economic welfare, is an obstinate survival from the times of the Economic Man. The presumption that the national product is the sole source of additions and alterations to people's economic welfare is the result of an implicit identification between 'economic' and 'productive' activity. The temptation to make some such identification would be obvious under conditions obtaining in the world inhabited by the Economic Man. In such a world, the production possibility curve will exhaust the enterprise and ingenuity of the community. And for such a community the criterion of achievement in the economic sense in every line of rational endeavour will be the same: a change in the size and shape of the national income. In such a set-up, presumably, the poet, the scientist, the thinker, the seer, all would be brooding over a single obsession: the Net National Product! Fortunately, however, it is not necessary to define economics in the setting of a mono-maniac's world. It is not necessary to insist that the end towards which all economic activity is directed must be so much output; or that the eventual tangible result of such activity can only be so much capital formation and so much consumption.

Even if human effort were solely directed towards the raising of a football team or changing the social structure, or simply following one policy rather than another, provided only that the capacity for making such effort is limited, it would deserve to be considered as economic activity. 'The economist,' as Lionel Robbins had said, 'is not concerned with ends as such. He is concerned with the way in which the attainment of ends is limited. The ends may be noble or they may be base. They may be "material" or "immaterial"— if ends can be so described. But if the attainment of one set of ends involves the sacrifice of others, then it has an economic aspect.'[1]

It follows that it is rather pointless to try to imagine distinctions between economic and other forms of welfare merely on the basis of distinctions between the national product and the other (material or non-material) end-results of purposeful human activity. It is only a confusion between ends and means which has prompted people to conceive of *targets* which could be described as 'economic' and 'non-economic' and to try to delimit welfare economics to the pursuit of the former to the exclusion of the latter. 'The habit, prevalent among certain groups of economists,' as Robbins had observed long ago, 'of discussing "economic satisfactions" is alien to the central

[1] *An Essay on the Nature and Significance of Economic Science*, Second Edition, Macmillan, London, 1935, p. 25.

intention of economic analysis.'[1] But the habit has died hard.

There is one particular sense, however, in which the term 'economic welfare' can continue to have operational significance. It hardly needs to be pointed out that certain *aspects* of human welfare (no discrete *part* of it) cannot be stated in principle as end-results of policy. Those aspects of welfare which bear no estimable relation to rationalised effort are obviously beyond the scope of economic analysis. By 'economic welfare', therefore, we may choose to define not a portion of general welfare, but certain tangible aspects of it which are capable of being described in terms of choice of ends and scarcity of means; and it is precisely in this redefined sense that the term reappears in Post-Pigovian welfare economics.[2]

[1] *The Nature and Significance of Economic Science*, p. 25.
[2] See, for example, I. M. D. Little, *A Critique of Welfare Economics*, Oxford, Clarendon Press, p. 6.

CHAPTER II

The Meaning of Welfare Perception

I

In the theory of economic welfare two rather fundamental questions must be taken as settled from the
outside. Whatever happen to be the actual answers to
these,[1] they would be irrelevant to the precise nature of our
inquiry.

The first question obviously is, 'What is welfare?' Any
answer to such a question would no doubt involve value
judgment of one kind or another and would therefore be
relevant to economics only as a datum imported into the
system. How ever much the ends of human welfare be presented in terms of economic aggregates such as output,
etc., the decision to follow such an end is essentially a kind
of ethical judgment which must be beyond the scope of
economics.

The second question would be, 'How is welfare perceived?' The answer to this particular question does not
necessarily involve a value-decision. Nevertheless, it
should undoubtedly be disciplines other than economics
to which a study of the *process* of welfare perception would
be relevant.

The question, therefore, to which we as economists

[1] And these answers can be, if we may say so without seeming unduly to
indulge in bits of amateur philosophy and psychology, rather remarkably
inconclusive!

must now address ourselves, takes the first two stages involved in its formulation for granted. Consequently, we merely ask, 'When do we assume or presume that welfare (however defined) has been perceived by the individual (whatever the exact physiological or psychological process involved)?'

Before we may proceed to examine the problem of welfare identification raised by our question, we must make an explicit admission; it is that an important axiom is implied in our statement of the problem itself. We shall stand by it for the rest of our analysis. There would, therefore, exist a certain bias throughout the study, originating from this, our primary axiom.

In simple terms, the axiom is 'that the welfare of any individual is what that individual perceives it to be'. This may appear at first sight to be pretty obvious, until one realises that a rigorous application of this principle would exclude from our field of analysis certain conclusions of some of the dominant systems of social and political philosophy.[1] It should be realised, however, that our axiom does not go contrary to any particular form of economic, social or political organisation. It only requires that the state of welfare, in so far as it can be judged at all, has to be judged strictly and primarily in terms of welfare perception of the individual.

It may be somewhat important also to point out that our axiom is not identical with the more assertive and positive axiom of nineteenth-century individualism: 'that the indi-

[1] Welfare economics based on alternative axioms is not only possible, but has also been known to have been quite fashionable ever since the days of Plato ('the philosopher-kings') and Aristotle ('the Natural Law'). Contemporary references are, of course, unnecessary.

vidual *alone* knows *what* increases or lessens his welfare.' In other words, we have presumed no necessary knowledge on the part of the individual which would give him any competence to judge *except* by results. What we have assumed to be beyond question, however, is that the consequence to an individual, of the end-result of an action, that individual alone is competent to judge.

Our axiom does not rule out social intervention even of the most positive form. But to judge the results of any such intervention, or of any other form of activity for the matter of that, from the point of view of welfare, we resolve to go by the perception of the individual.

In our analytical framework, therefore, the unit of account is the individual, which in all cases would be 'prior' to the group. The primary 'myth' in our model, that is to say, is the individual; the social or the group myth emerges either as the function of the individual or not at all.

II

Granted that the individual is assumed to play the primary role in welfare perception, our problem is reduced to one of devising a meaningful definition of a state in which welfare can be said to have been perceived. So long as the attainment of satisfaction or the enjoyment of utility is described *purely* in terms of introspection, no statement about the state of welfare can be subjected to the test of refutability. Any such statement, therefore, being in principle neither verifiable nor falsifiable would be meaningless from the point of view of scientific method. We hasten to add that, of course, any such statement may be completely true. It is only that a hypothesis, with whatever degree of intuitive certainty it may be held, would still be lacking in operational significance if it could not be disproved *if wrong*. We can, therefore, admit only such propositions as are contradictable, at least in principle.

We may recall at this stage that we had narrowed down our definition of economic welfare in the last chapter by insisting on having only those aspects of welfare which could be stated as economic targets. If, however, we wish to restrict ourselves strictly to a definition which would be completely 'meaningful' in the sense discussed above, a further qualification seems to be necessary. Because only those aspects of 'economic welfare' (as hitherto defined) about which consumer preference, etc. could be expressed in the form of refutable hypotheses, could be said to be falling within the methodological boundaries set by us.

Our 'operational' definition of economic welfare, therefore, now becomes necessarily subjected to a double constraint. On the one hand it requires, as we have already seen in Chapter I, that the content of welfare be capable of being described in terms of targets attainable through economic means. On the other hand, following our argument above, economic welfare needs to be so defined as to make it possible for statements made about it by the individual to be testable at least in principle. To be precise, the first requirement is concerned with what makes up the material content of welfare; the second takes into account what makes the identification of economic welfare a meaningful concept. All aspects of general welfare which do not depend in principle on attainment of ends through

c   M.U.

economic means, have to be excluded from our consideration because of the first constraint. Any aspect of economic
welfare which does not permit of being experienced solely
in an observable way, similarly has to be dismissed because of the second. To take an obvious example, the degree of 'contentment' would perhaps constitute an aspect
of welfare quite outside our field of enquiry, on account of
the requirement that the content of an admissible aspect
of welfare has to be stated in the form of ends which can be
attained, at least in principle, through economic means.
Similarly, a general 'widening' of the capacity to enjoy
the material things of life, for example, may well be an
aspect of economic welfare which also would be inadmissible from our point of view, because of the requirement that statements about it must be capable of being
tested.

It may be interesting to notice the part played in the
present context by the axiom of individual freedom which
we introduced in the preceding section. If welfare were not
assumed to be essentially the concern of the individual, and
if, for example, a criterion for determining changes in
welfare could without difficulty be borrowed ready-to-use
from a specified set of social codes, then, of course, the second
constraint on the definition of economic welfare proposed
above would be somewhat trivial. Because in such a situation neither a change in taste, nor a possible change in the
state of civilisation of the individual would make judgment on the state of welfare any the more difficult. Given
a built-in set of welfare norms the ascertainment of the
actual level of welfare would no longer be the individual's
affair.

III

Having laid down the requirement of refutability as the basis of making admissible propositions about economic welfare, we may now turn once again to the question of welfare perception. It would be evident that so long as the perception of welfare is not assumed to be a guide to observable activity on the part of the individual, no possible hypothesis can be advanced about it in refutable form. Therefore, whether generally true or not, we are forced to accept the assumption, at least as our starting point, that there exists a positive correspondence between welfare and intended behaviour of the individual. In other words, we rule out for the time being the possibility that some people might quite rationally (deliberately) construct their scales of preferences without reference to what they consider to be in their best interest. Or else, we assume that if there is a conflict between the individual's tastes and his values, we resolve to look at him only after he has made up his mind to follow either the one or the other. By this simple resolution we propose to bridge the gap between the individual's perception of welfare and his intentions, i.e., his preferences.[1]

Once it is accepted that the above-mentioned assumption of a positive correspondence between welfare perception and preference is a necessary prerequisite for making useful statements about the state of welfare, an interesting conclusion seems immediately to follow.

[1] There would still remain, it may be noticed, a second gap: that between preferences and actual behaviour (choice). While the first may involve a discrepancy between values and tastes, the second may be apparent in a discrepancy between tastes and expediency. (Cf. Chapter I, p. 8, specially footnote 1; also appendix: 'Choice and Revealed Preference'.)

Without intruding into the question of the *nature* of welfare perception (which we opted to rule out of our field of enquiry), we may nevertheless observe that an individual's recognition of a welfare (or any other) situation can be of two possible kinds: he may recognise a state of welfare *absolutely*, or may recognise it only in a *comparative* sense (as better or worse than some other situation). In other words, the individual may perceive a situation as good or bad independently of comparisons, or he may not. *But whatever be the nature of welfare perception on the plane of introspection, any meaningful statement about it must take the same form: it must be in terms of comparison.* There can be no particular sense in saying for example, that an individual has attained some (specified or unspecified degree of) satisfaction in a situation unless we have in mind also some other situation in which he would attain more (or less) satisfaction. When we say that 'there can be no sense', we mean of course, that 'there can be made no economic use of the "knowledge" contained' in a statement of 'absolute' perception of welfare or satisfaction. The meaninglessness of absolute perception of welfare is therefore on the plane of economic operations only and need not be on any other (say, physical, psychological or philosophical) plane.

The only (economically) meaningful description of the individual's welfare perception that can be made, has to be of the form: 'satisfaction is greater (or less) at the situation *A* than at the situation *B*.' And this would be quite irrespective of whether in fact the individual can perceive the two situations independently or only in a comparative order.

We must hasten to add, however, that contrary to what

may perhaps be intuitively expected, this requirement
that an economically meaningful statement about welfare
perception has to be a comparative statement has nothing
(or very little) to do with the so-called cardinal-ordinal
controversy. As we shall be arguing in the following
chapter, the question of measurement of welfare can be
quite distinct from that of its identification. Nothing pre-
cludes a cardinalist, for example, from assuming that welfare perception is essentially one of comparative differences
and then holding that these differences are uniquely
measurable.[1] Similarly nothing prevents the ordinalist
from contesting the measurability of these differences in
quantitative terms and yet holding that a state of welfare
can be apprehended through introspection without having
to make comparisons at all. That the opposite, in either
case, is usually true is the product of a temperamental
rather than a logical necessity.

We have now been able to make one fundamental proposition regarding the meaning of welfare perception in
economics. It is simply that regardless of the actual nature
of welfare or of welfare perception, any (economically
meaningful) hypothesis about the state of welfare must be
based on a comparison, i.e., on an ordering of given
situations. As economists, we can set about the question
of welfare perception only when more than one situation
is described *at least* in better-or-worse terms. Therefore,

[1] The assumption of relative perception does seem to preclude, however,
the more orthodox variant of cardinalism, which regards utility as measurable in the sense of being *addible*. It can be consistent, we may observe, only
with a less uncompromising cardinalist notion, e.g., that utility is measurable up to a linear transformation. Cf. A. A. Alchian, 'The Meaning of
Utility Measurement', *American Economic Review*, 1953.

an economic definition of welfare or utility implies
essentially at least ordinal measurability.[1]

IV

We shall now turn to what may be described as a procedural problem involved in the definition of 'meaningfulness' of welfare perception. It is evident that as soon as we
introduce the principle of 'refutability', we undertake to
make a resolution as to what should constitute for us satisfactory refutation (or rather, *absence* of refutation) of a
given proposition. We shall see that to make any such resolution involves an element of decision (and therefore,
logically, an element of arbitrariness), and in consequence,
differences on the question are bound to exist.

Differences on what constitutes refutability can be due
to (*a*) differences (alleged or actual) in the *nature* of the
propositions advanced; or (*b*) a genuine difference on a
question of methodology.

[1] The well-known controversy as to whether utility can be taken to be
cardinally measurable, really poses an *additional* question as to whether the
differences between situations which can be placed in order are more precisely measurable. Cardinalism, therefore, does not provide an *alternative*
hypothesis; it needs an additional one. This, as we shall see later, has
allowed the use of the 'Occam's razor' by the ordinalist.

We may best pose the measurability question thus: Utility implies at
least ordinal measurability (i.e., measurability unique only up to a monotonic transformation). Can a further precision be made (i.e., a further restriction be imposed) which would be both meaningful and justifiable?

We have no alternative but to use 'cardinalism' as a round term for the
various hypotheses which answer the above question, in one way or the
other, in the affirmative. Thus Robertson, the Marshallian ('utility can be
added') and Friedman, the Positivist ('utility is measurable up to a linear
transformation') have both been described (and no doubt, would describe
themselves) as Cardinalists.

See, M. Friedman and L. J. Savage, 'The Expected Utility Hypothesis
and the Measurability of Utility', *Journal of Political Economy*, 1952; D. H.
Robertson, 'Utility and All That', loc. cit.

So far as the first kind of differences are concerned, their character would quite easily be seen. In the circumstances, for example, in which a proposition can be subjected to laboratory control, as would often be the case in the natural sciences, refutability of hypotheses would surely be related to an experimental procedure. A suitably designed experiment, may therefore understandably be judged adequate to test the Law of Falling Bodies. Similarly, in the circumstances in which a statement can be regarded as a forecast, refutation would evidently mean the eventual falsification of the forecast. Statements about the perception of welfare, however, cannot be controlled either by laboratory experiments or by the passage of time (except in very trivial instances). The procedure of testing hypotheses in welfare theory must, therefore, be somewhat more arbitrary and less certain than the procedures often open to the natural sciences.

The second kind of differences on what constitutes refutability can be related to the well-known controversy in methodology between the adherents of the 'operationalist' and the 'hypothetico-deductive' schools which has now managed to spread into the realm of economics also.[1] It

[1] For expositions of the operationalist standpoint in economics see T. W. Hutchison, *The Significance and Basic Postulates of Economic Theory*, London, Macmillan, and Milton Friedman, *Essays in Positive Economics*, University of Chicago Press. The assertion of the hypothetico-deductive method has often been casual (or only implicit) and is hard to be found in a formally rigorous presentation. The best exposition of the point of view, to our knowledge, is contained in F. H. Knight's, ' "What is Truth" in Economics' which is a review of Hutchison's work (loc. cit.) published in the *Journal of Political Economy*, February 1940 and reprinted in *On the History and Method of Economics* by Frank H. Knight, University of Chicago Press. See also, reprinted in the same volume, his, 'Salvation by Science: The Gospel according to Professor Lundberg' from the *Journal of Political Economy*, December 1947.

will be our contention that it is only in the context of this broad methodological question that the full significance of the measurability controversy in utility theory can properly be realised.

To decide what constitutes refutability of a proposition, it is possible to follow any one of two alternative rules of procedure. In the first place, we may resolve to admit a proposition if and only if it is *itself* observable (thus making it directly falsifiable if untrue). This would be the Operationalist resolution. In the second place, we may resolve to admit a hypothesis only if (*a*) at least *some* consequences deducible from it are observable (i.e., directly falsifiable); and (*b*) that no other more 'economical' hypothesis (i.e., one depending on a smaller number of assumptions to explain the same consequences or the same assumptions to explain a larger number of consequences) exists. And this would be the Hypothetico-deductive resolution.

It is clear that the operationalist resolution excludes any proposition which does not describe an event (i.e., which is not immediately 'instantial'). It has, therefore, no use for general explanatory hypotheses which play a vital part in the hypothetico-deductive method.

The most brilliant two-sentence assertion of the method we have come across is due to Hicks, casually thrown in, while discussing the role of his indifference-preference hypothesis:

'The assumption of behaviour according to a scale of preferences comes in here as the simplest hypothesis, not necessarily the only possible hypothesis, but the one which, initially at least, seems to be the most sensible hypothesis to try. Its status is identically the same as that of a well-known class of hypotheses in natural science, hypotheses which cannot be tested directly, but which can be used for the arrangement of empirical data in meaningful ways, and which are accepted or rejected according to their success or failure as instruments of arrangement.' (J. R. Hicks in *A Revision of Demand Theory,* Oxford at the Clarendon Press, 1956, p. 17.)

The operationalist resolution in utility theory leads to positivist-behaviourism of the type of which Samuelson (among the ordinalists) and Friedman (among the cardinalists) are the leading exponents. Similarly, the hypothetico-deductive resolution accounts for the introspectionist approach which lies in the tradition of Alfred Marshall, and of which Hicks (among the ordinalists) and Armstrong (among the cardinalists) are the modern champions.

To point out that methodologically, the choice among the two alternative procedural resolutions is *not* determinable from purely *a priori* considerations (and, therefore, in that particular sense, *must be arbitrary*), is merely to assert that we, as economists, must make the choice on known *factual* considerations. The arbitrariness, we must remember, is that of facts and not (quite) that of (the economist's) tastes.

We have tried to present the Measurability problem in utility theory in the context of these basic methodological alternatives.[1] We have also indicated our choice. It has been our conclusion that the behaviourist method has failed to produce theorems in utility theory which can cover the same operational range as the theorems enunciated by introspective explanatory hypotheses. It has failed, that is to say, on factual considerations alone; which leaves aside the question of taste[2] which must in any case determine whether 'explanations' are by themselves not worth having.

[1] For a brief final account of our methodological argument, see Chapter X, specially Section IV.

[2] We have not tried to hide — in fact we have tried to emphasise — that we, on our part, are inclined to the rule of including explanatory propositions from considerations of taste alone.

V

We conclude our observations on the meaning of welfare perception by offering one more comment. The validity of the behaviourist procedure of admitting only those propositions about the state of welfare which are made strictly in terms of immediately observable behaviour, is itself dependent on the celebrated Samuelsonian axiom of Revealed Preference. To argue from behaviour to welfare is to take the link between choice and preference for granted. Without assuming this link there can be no behaviourist welfare theory at all. But this link itself is not observable; it is therefore axiomatic.[1]

In the usual circumstances the assumption that behaviour reflects preference on the part of the individual concerned is no doubt the only sensible one that we can make. Not only does it seem to command intuitive support, its invalidation would provide a good definition of irrational behaviour in normal circumstances. But we have already observed[2] that there can be situations the relation between which the individual can clearly comprehend at the level of introspection, but which nevertheless he cannot express at the level of *immediate* behaviour. One such situation would be the existence of 'indifference', which the behaviourist (unless prepared to introduce fresh procedural rules for describing behaviour statistically) has to rule out straight away! Another would be, as we have seen, the existence of non-comparability (which, of course,

[1] Note, however, that the behaviourist-cardinalist in utility theory has avoided this methodological predicament by opting out of 'welfare' theory altogether!

[2] See Chapter I above, p. 8.

we do not expect to come across very often). In both types of situations *some* choice will be made which will not reveal (the absence of) preference.

Rational choice in the two types of situations referred to above, is indeterminate. We offer an instance below in which choice (assuming rationality) is determinate, *and* owing to considerations of a game-theory type, it is *necessarily* contrary to assumed preferences.[1]

Let us consider a community of three individuals, A, F, G, who are faced with a collective choice from four alternative ends M, N, O, P. Let us assume that the community has resolved to make all decisions as to the choice of ends by a majority vote. The three individuals, let us suppose, perceive the states of welfare associated with M, N, O and P in the following order, the direction of preference being to the left:

A: N, O, P, M F: M, N, O, P G: P, O, N, M

Let us further assume, for the sake of simplicity, that the task of proposing a particular end for the community's consideration is habitually left to F and G, who are therefore, *both* 'sponsors' and 'choosers' in our model, while A is 'chooser', i.e., voter only.

It can easily be shown that in a vote, whichever of the two 'sponsors' puts up his best 'candidate' (i.e., reveals his actual preference) first, loses. For example, if F sets up M for the community's approval, G can set up P and win; while if G is trapped into putting up P *first*, F can sponsor N and win!

[1] A more elaborate model has been set up and analysed in an Appendix, 'Choice and Revealed Preference', in which the determinate solution is represented as an ordinal version of the well known 'saddle-point theorem' in the Theory of Games.

In the above voting situation the sponsor F will clearly be better advised *not* to reveal his first preference in actual behaviour. If he puts up M, as we have seen, the result is the victory for P, which is the worst that can happen to him. If, however, he sponsors his second preference N, then his opponent has no answer to it, and he wins the support of the majority. Thus the rational solution of the problem to F is that if he has to proceed without the knowledge of what G might be doing, he should *choose N rather than M*, thus *reversing* his order of preferences.

Conditions under which the correspondence between observed behaviour and actual preference does not necessarily exist, are also conditions under which the Samuelson-type welfare theory becomes useless. It is no doubt true that the idea of an act of choice revealing the individual's ordering of situations in welfare terms is not peculiar to the Samuelsonian system alone. In the Hicksian introspectionist procedure also, as indeed in traditional Marshallian theory the same assumption is relied upon. Nevertheless, the position of the assumption is not nearly as important and as necessary to the introspectionist as it no doubt is to the behaviourist. The *usual* implication of a statement of preference order in the manner of Hicks is of course that the individual's observed equilibrium would be consistent with it. But the conceptual validity (as different from immediate usefulness) of Hicksian welfare theory does not depend on that implication. Moreover in situations where observed behaviour is known to imply nothing, introspection, however inadequate, remains the only sensible guide to welfare policy.

CHAPTER III

Welfare Perception and
Measurability Question

I

We have discussed some of the problems connected with the economic definition of welfare
perception. We may now turn our attention to a
somewhat more controversial (and, for our purpose, the
crucial) subject: that of measurability of utility. Positions
normally taken up on this question are almost completely
polarised into the two great contending camps of 'cardinalism' and 'ordinalism'. Before we embark upon an
examination of the actual controversy, however, we hope
to be able to lay down an important first principle, which
should help us resolve this issue a little further. In order to
derive this first principle we propose to dwell upon the admissibility of a simple distinction in welfare theory: that
between perception and measurement of welfare.

The distinction between the question of perception or
identification and that of measurement may appear at
first sight to be straightforward enough. To discern the
existence of a given welfare situation, for example, and to
assess and measure it, should generally appear to be two
distinct and successive logical stages in the entire process of
the individual's comprehension of that situation. We shall
find, however, that this distinction does not exist in every

possible case: a consideration which has an important bearing on the entire cardinal-ordinal controversy.

On more than one occasion in the preceding pages, we have made the observation that the nature of welfare perception in the physiological or psychological sense is necessarily beyond the scope of our discipline. It is indeed of the utmost importance that we should remember and observe this limitation placed upon our field of enquiries. Nevertheless, as we shall presently notice, it is also necessary to recognise that different hypotheses regarding the act of welfare perception (hypotheses, which by themselves can be tested through procedures open only to other sciences, for example, through psychological experimentation, and which must be regarded as given from the 'outside' by us), may postulate essentially different conceptual relationships between the discernment and the measurement of welfare. We have considered below the two alternative hypotheses regarding a particular act of discernment which one can possibly make, and have tried to clarify the consequence of each so far as the question of measurability is concerned. For reasons already made obvious, we have not tried to pronounce upon the relative merits (or validity) of either hypothesis.[1]

[1] We are tempted to quote from Moore, in this connection, an extract which has already (in a slightly different context) been brought to the notice of fellow-economists by Dr. W. D. Lamont (*The Value Judgement*, Edinburgh University Press, 1956, p. 7):

'. . . it is necessary to consider what things are such that, if they existed by themselves, in absolute isolation, we should yet judge their existence to be good.'

And then,

'. . . in order to decide upon the relative degrees of value of different things, we must similarly consider what comparative value seems to attach to the isolated existence of each.' (*Principia Ethica*, par. 112.)

II

It would appear on reflection that only two possible hypotheses can be advanced about the nature of discernment or identification of a particular situation. According to the first hypothesis, the individual would be thought of as being able to identify a given situation in *isolation*, without reference to the existence of other situations; according to the second, he would be able to recognise a situation only in so far as he could place it in a relationship with other situations. While an act of comparison would be an essential part of identification under the latter hypothesis, it would play no necessary rôle under the former.

Applied to welfare theory, this of course means that if the first hypothesis is admitted, the individual would be deemed capable of being aware of a welfare situation without having to compare it with other situations. Thus he would know a particular state to be good or bad, say, without encountering the possibility of better or worse states. The second hypothesis would permit him, however, to recognise a particular state only *inside* a ranking order, i.e., only as better or worse than other states. The first type of identification would be absolute, and the second type only relative.

When we refer to physical things, we imply the admissibility of the first type of hypothesis about their identification. Thus, the leg of a chair, an amount of money and a mountain are all expected to have this in common that a direct cognition of each is possible. The physical means of welfare, like all physical things, are

surely identifiable absolutely and in isolation. But there is
no *a priori* grounds for believing that the same would be
true of the identification of welfare itself in the individual's
mind. Needless to add perhaps, that there is similarly no *a
priori* reason why welfare should *not* be identifiable in the
individual's mind entirely in isolation. It will be our
object below to demonstrate that the first hypothesis
leaves the controversy on welfare measurability completely unresolved, while the second is fatal to a particular
(and perhaps the 'popular') notion of 'cardinal' measurability of welfare.

We shall complete our demonstration in two steps. We
shall first clarify the meanings of 'ordinal' and 'cardinal'
measurement of utility. Secondly, we shall observe the
implications of each of the two alternative hypotheses of
welfare perception for the cardinal-ordinal question.

III

Ordinal measurability implies that only the direction
(i.e., the sign) of a change in welfare is ascertainable.
Thus, if the individual is faced with a number of alternative situations, say, A, B, C, D and E, then the levels of
welfare associated with each of these situations would be
ordinally measurable if these can be ranked by the individual in order of preference. Given the ranking, we are en-
titled to use a set of numbers to denote the ranking order.
Thus we may attribute the number 7, say to the highest
ranked and 0 (zero) to the lowest and other numbers in between for the other situations. In this manner we can easily
express a set of ordinally ranked situations in terms of
numbers, as for example, in the following table:

Situation	Ranking order	Number attributed
D	1	7
A	2	5
B	3	4
C	4	2
E	5	0

But the numbers on the right-hand side have only one significance: that they decrease with a fall in the ranking order. Therefore, they could be replaced by *any* other set of numbers which has this property, i.e., which gives a smaller number for a less preferred situation, as in the following table:

Ranking order	Number attributed			
	(a)	(b)	(c)	(d)
1	7	37	25	11111
2	5	36	24	1111
3	4	35	23	111
4	2	13	22	11
5	0	1	2	1

Any set of numbers which retains in this manner the direction of change (i.e., the signs of the first differences) shown in any other set is said to be a 'monotonic' transformation of it. Ordinal measurability can therefore be defined as measurability up to a monotonic transformation.

If we choose to limit the meaning of ordinality simply to measurability up to monotonic transformations, then the problem of defining 'cardinal' measurement becomes simple enough: any type of measurement which implies more precision (restriction) than simple ordinality can then be called cardinal measurement.

D

It should at once be clear that a precise definition of ordinality (such as the one we considered above) must leave the definition of cardinality somewhat imprecise (and *vice versa*). Granting that measurement (by definition) can be either cardinal or ordinal, it follows that as soon as we define one (and only one) particular type of relative measure as ordinal (cardinal) *all other* possible types are residually defined to be cardinal (ordinal).

In course of our survey of the cardinal-ordinal controversy we shall find that while the ordinalists stick to the simple notion of measurability of utility up to monotone transformations (implying thereby that only the direction of a change in welfare carries operational significance), the cardinalists have explicitly or implicitly differed amongst themselves on what they really mean by measurability of utility.

Of the many possible meanings that can be given to 'cardinality,' when defined residually as 'more-than-ordinal-measurability', we shall be specifically concerned with only two. The first would be the Marshallian notion, championed, amongst others, by Robertson. It would simply involve the idea that utility is quantifiable, in the sense of being *addible*.[1] To say, according to the Marshallian definition, that the individual enjoys 8 units of welfare in one situation, for example, and 4 units in another, would amount to saying that the individual is twice as well-off in the former situation as he would be in the latter. This rather uncompromising definition of utility-

[1] 'Addibility' of utility, it should be noted, does not necessarily imply the further cardinalist assumption viz., addibility of utility *between persons*. The latter needs over and above 'addibility', also inter-personal comparability.

measurability, if we may say so, represents the cardinalist orthodoxy.

The second definition is due to the 'neo-cardinalists', following Morgenstern and Neumann and Milton Friedman,[1] who are, however, reluctant to concede any 'welfare content' to their definition of utility at all. Utility, according to them, is merely the name for a description of economic behaviour apparent in choice. Acts of choice can be so described as to clarify not only how the individual chooses one thing rather than another (which would yield simple ordinal measurement), but also how *strongly* (defined as how *frequently*) he makes the same choice (and which would therefore give the signs of the *second* differences as well). Such a precise description of choice implies the measurability of 'utility' up to a linear transformation.

Measurability up to a linear transformation is measurability which is unique except for the choice of an arbitrary origin and scale. It is certainly more precise than simple ordinal measurability but not very much more.[2] It involves the knowledge of the sign(s) of the first differences (which would be implicit in measurability up to monotonic transformations) as well as the sign(s) of the second differences.[3] The sign of a first difference tells us, as we can readily see, of the *direction* of preference. The sign of a second difference compares two acts of pre-

[1] See Chapter VIII below.

[2] Temperature, which is measurable except for arbitrary origin and scale (i.e., up to a linear transformation), is, for example, described by physicists as a *state* (as distinguished, say, from *amounts* of heat measured in calories): a clearly *ordinal concept*.

[3] The second differences may be defined as marginal utilities (which then are only *ordinally measurable*).

ference: it tells us whether preference in one case is stronger or weaker than in the other. It tells us something, therefore, of the *intensity* of preferences. In the following table, three different sets of numbers are used. Since each set gives the same signs of first and second differences as any of the others, the three sets are linear transformations of one another. If the signs of the first and second differences (i.e., the *directions* and *intensities*) of the preferences are as depicted, then each of the three sets of numbers (or any other linear transformation thereof) would be a correct measure of the preferences.

Situation	Sign of 1st difference	Sign of 2nd difference	Number attributed (a)	(b)	(c)
E			0	5	100
C	+		3	9	110
B	+	+	12	21	140
A	+	−	15	25	150
D	+	+	30	45	200

IV

As soon as we are clear in our minds about the meaning of 'cardinal' and 'ordinal' measurability, the implications of the absolute-discernment and the relative-discernment hypotheses become evident. In the first place, we discover that cardinal measurability in the orthodox Marshallian sense must imply absolute discernment. For surely if any state is quantitatively measurable, then it would at once become capable of being identified by that absolute measure *without* reference to any other states. We cannot, therefore, talk of 'amounts' of welfare when welfare itself is supposed to be perceived only in a comparative sense. In other words, the hypothesis of relative discernment of welfare is incompatible with the orthodox version of 'cardinalism'.

In the second place, while absolute (i.e., Marshallian) Cardinalism implies absolute discernment, the converse is not true. To be accurate, absolute discernment does not necessarily imply *any* measurability at all. The proposition that an individual can recognise 'happiness', for example, in isolation, does *not* imply an admission that happiness can be measured (or compared) in any manner whatsoever. The hypothesis of absolute identifiability of welfare leaves the question of measurability completely open. If a state is found to be absolutely discernible, it is to be seen whether it is also measurable; if it *is* also measurable, it is still to be seen how the measurement can be made: a consideration which can be illustrated as follows.

Let us conceive of a state *B*, say, which can be recognised without reference to states such as *A* and *C*. To take an illustration from life, *B* may be the boiling point of water, and *A* and *C* two other degrees of temperature. It is not necessary to compare *B* and *A* or *B* and *C* in order to be able to identify *B*, since *B* is uniquely associated with a precisely defined physical phenomenon, viz., boiling of water under certain conditions. But *B* in our illustration cannot be *measured in an additive sense*. It cannot be measured, that is to say, except in comparison to *A* or *C*. Thus the measurement of 100° C. would depend on comparison with other states while the precise identification of it is possible independently of any such comparison.

Had *B* referred to an amount of heat instead of a degree of warmth in our illustration, it would then have been amenable to quantitative measurement without reference to states such as *A* or *C*. In other words, an absolutely identifiable state *may* be measurable in quantitative terms; but it may just as well be not so uniquely measurable; and it is rather safe to remember that sometimes it may not be measurable at all.

Finally, we may observe that if a state is discernible only in the relative sense, then measurement must have entered into the act of discernment by definition. To take another example from life, when we talk of a state *B*, say, being warmer than *C* and cooler than *A*, we are able to recognise the three states individually only within the ranking order *A*, *B*, *C*; which also shows their *ordinal* measurability. If we are also able to perceive whether the difference in warmth between *A* and *B* is more (or less) pronounced than that between *B* and *C*, then that would imply measurability in the *neo-cardinal* sense. Given relative discernibility, the states *will be* measurable some way or other (but *will not* be measurable in a quantitative sense).

We may now sum up our observations by advancing the following propositions which have emerged in course of our argument:

(*a*) Welfare, when identifiable, may be either absolutely discernible or discernible only relatively.

(*b*) When absolutely discernible, welfare may or may not be measurable.

(*c*) When welfare is absolutely discernible *and* measurable, it may be either quantifiable or only capable of being compared (in one or more ways).

(*d*) When welfare is only relatively discernible, it must be measurable but cannot be quantifiable.

Therefore, to conclude, while the hypothesis of absolute discernment of welfare is neutral between cardinalism and ordinalism, that of relative discernment rules out orthodox cardinalism by definition. However, from *a priori* considerations alone, the acceptance of one or the other of the hypotheses must remain, to the economist, largely a question of taste and temperament.

PART II

THE MEASURABILITY CONTROVERSY

CHAPTER IV

The Measurability Controversy

The controversy between cardinalist and ordinalist approaches to utility theory is not of recent origin. Nevertheless, it is only in the past few years that the methodological and other issues involved in the dispute have gained a certain degree of prominence. We suggested elsewhere that it is quite possible to pursue this intriguing question beyond the frontiers of economic science. An example may now serve to emphasise this possibility, and indicate our line of procedure.

Let us suppose that we are confronted with a particular brand of ordinalist theory which is derived from the hypothesis of relative discernment of welfare, with which we have been already made familiar in the last chapter. And let us suppose that we also encounter a certain cardinal-utility theory built around the assumption of absolute discernment. Now surely some of the very fundamental differences between the two formulations of utility theory which we may wish to consider would follow from a dispute, the origin of which is no longer (or perhaps not yet) within the scope and method of economics? We must not lose sight of the principle, however, that questions which do not fall within the scope and method of economics, whatever their importance may be in another context, are not economic questions and are therefore irrelevant to our purpose.

Since the possibility of being involved in 'extra-territorial' disputes by no means belongs only to limiting cases, we have to confine ourselves, so far as the present study is concerned, explicitly to those aspects of the measurability question which can be handled by tools that economics can fashion.

It will be our object to examine in the following pages the principal cardinal and ordinal formulations in utility theory; and it will be our method to subject certain basic propositions involved in these formulations to a number of indirect tests for refutation. We shall take up, for example, the well-known theorem on inverse price-demand relationship. We shall examine the relative efficiency and acceptability of each particular version of the theorem as it appears in (a) the Marshallian marginal-utility theory, (b) the Hicksian indifference-preference theory, and (c) Samuelson's Revealed Preference analysis. We shall, however, propose certain different tests for the other two formulations of utility theory which we shall be investigating. The first is the Marginal-Preference theory of W. E. Armstrong, and the second, the statistical-utility theory of Neumann-Morgenstern and their followers.

The reason for contemplating a different treatment for Armstrong's theory lies simply in the fact that at least in its most recent form,[1] the theory is intended primarily to provide a solution to the group-welfare problem, and not particularly to facilitate demand analysis. The reason for the departure in the second case is similar. Those who believe in the experimental verifiability of a Morgenstern-

---

[1] W. E. Armstrong, 'Utility and the Theory of Welfare', *Oxford Economic Papers*, October 1951.

Neumann type cardinal-utility hypothesis, are interested in the expounding of a theory of consistent consumer behaviour in the presence of risk and do not feel committed either to a demand theorem, or, as we have already observed, to propositions of a welfare nature. That we have decided to include this last class of utility theory at all in our study, is principally on account of a conviction that notwithstanding the refusal of its exponents to be drawn into group-welfare theory, the importance of its assertions for a theory of individual welfare would probably be beyond dispute.

We have found it convenient to carry out our survey of the cardinal-ordinal controversy through five logically distinct stages. It will perhaps be noticed that our classification ties with our intention to distinguish between utility theories not only according to whether the cardinal or the ordinal hypothesis is used, but also according to whether the behaviourist or the introspectionist methodological resolution is adopted.[1] In the following chapters, therefore, we propose to proceed as follows:

Chapter V: The first stage — introspective cardinalist: the Marshallian Utility Theory.

Chapter VI: The second stage — introspective ordinalist: the Hicksian Indifference-Preference Theory.

Chapter VII: The third stage — behaviourist ordinalist: Samuelson's Revealed Preference Analysis.

Chapter VIII: The fourth stage — behaviourist cardinalist: the Morgenstern-Neumann Index.

[1] See Chapter II, Section IV above, specially, p. 27.

CHAPTER V

The Introspective Cardinalist

I

In the present chapter we intend to examine the Marshallian formulation of the marginal-utility theory, which we have described, it may be noticed, as both 'introspective' and cardinalist. The distinction between what we called the 'introspective' and the 'behaviourist' methods in advancing theoretical propositions in utility theory, it may be remembered, was touched upon by us on an earlier occasion.[1] It would, perhaps, not be out of place here to offer a further comment on the rôle of introspective hypotheses in utility theory.

The method of introspection permits us to look upon the behaviour of the individual as the product of a set of 'propensities', which (looking into ourselves), we attribute to him. The set of propensities would be by its very nature unobservable as well as variable. It is only the resultant behaviour that is observable. Assuming, however, that behaviour is not aimless but purposeful, the introspection of a propensity arising out of an imagined purpose is thought to be a useful procedural device. Obviously, direct empirical refutation of such a procedural abstraction is impossible. All that we can possibly do by way of testing it is to examine how far it is necessary for the derivation of

[1] See Chapter II, Section IV above.

meaningful (and valid) theorems which it claims to
enunciate. It is only in this indirect manner that some sort
of a judgment on an 'introspective' hypothesis is possible.

The concept of marginal utility with a number of properties ascribed to it appears in Marshallian theory as one
such 'introspective' procedural device. Its admissibility
rests entirely on its necessity.

The criterion of 'necessity' suggests that the marginal-
utility hypothesis (or any other similar introspective
hypothesis), in order that it may be admitted as a scientific
proposition, ought to satisfy three conditions: (i) that it
can enunciate with or without a number of subsidiary assumptions, a meaningful (i.e., one that can be refuted *if*
wrong) *and* valid (*i.e.*, one that has *not* been found wrong)
theorem; (ii) that no other meaningful theorem derived
from it on the same or fewer assumptions is in fact found
wrong; and (iii) that no alternative hypothesis is *known*
which can enunciate a more general theorem on the same
assumptions or the same theorem on fewer assumptions
(i.e., which is more 'economical').

Of the three conditions of admissibility of introspective
hypotheses, only the first is positive. Evidently the onus of
testing the two negative conditions cannot fairly lie on the
proponents of the hypothesis.

So far as the first of the two negative conditions are concerned, certainly as soon as a theorem enunciated from the
hypothesis concerned is falsified by observation, the hypothesis itself has to be discarded. But the *absence* of the
possibility that some theorem will in fact be falsified can
never be proved. In principle, therefore, we cannot fulfil
the condition except in the relative sense that its infringe-

ment has not been observed. The same would hold no doubt for the second negative condition too. However, its status as a criterion of admissibility of introspective hypotheses has to be established on a somewhat different plane and it therefore deserves a brief comment by itself.

The procedure of discarding an original hypothesis as soon as a new one is found which assumes less or explains more, does not imply that this entails a *falsification* of the original hypothesis. All that need be implied is that so long as we get the same results by assuming less or better results by making the same assumptions, the relatively simple or the more general explanation is to be admitted as a matter of procedure. The more complex or the less general explanation is to be rejected not because it is found to be invalid (which it assuredly is not), but because the validity of the older hypothesis has become operationally of no consequence and therefore irrelevant to our purpose. Hence it should be understood that if we decide (as we shall) to discard the Marshallian hypothesis on the ground that ordinal theory, with fewer assumptions to make, is found able to deduce all the theorems which cardinal theory can, then that decision is only part of one of our methodological procedural resolutions, and is *not* a verdict on the 'truth' or 'falsity' of the cardinal hypothesis. Rejection of the cardinal theory due to infringement of this last condition will, therefore, convey a different meaning from that implied in its rejection due to infringement of the other two conditions: it will be, that is, altogether on a different plane.

The theorem which the Marshallian hypothesis claims to enunciate is generally known as the Law of Demand.

'The greater the amount to be sold,' to quote the famous statement of the 'law', 'the smaller must be the price at which it is offered in order that it may find purchasers; or, in other words, the amount demanded increases with a fall in price, and diminishes with a rise in price.'[1] It is to an examination of this 'law' that we must turn for a test of the cardinal utility hypothesis.

II

It is possible to derive the Marshallian demand theorem in two stages. In the first, we make a number of assumptions regarding the *nature* of marginal utility; and in the second we make a particular assumption about, what we may call for want of a better name, the *behaviour* of marginal utility. We are concerned in the present section only with the first stage of the argument, reserving the second stage until the next section.

Two important assumptions about the nature of utility are implied in the Marshallian theory. The first is that an increment in utility (i.e., marginal utility) is quantifiable in principle. This assumption is the basis of the orthodox cardinalist approach to utility measurement and as we may recall, it at once commits the cardinalist to a more fundamental hypothesis: that utility or welfare is capable of absolute and independent discernment. We have already demonstrated that while this latter hypothesis is perfectly compatible with a purely ordinal view of utility, the alternative hypothesis of relative identifiability of welfare definitely rules out quantifiability. The cardinalist, therefore, is found to be in a rather unenviable position at

[1] Alfred Marshall, *Principles of Economics*, Eighth Edition, p. 99.

the start of the controversy. The onus of winning us over to the hypothesis of absolute identifiability of welfare lies squarely on his shoulders, while the ordinalist can choose to remain comfortably aloof and view his opponent's efforts impartially, since his own position is not affected whatever be the outcome.

To come back to the assumption of quantifiability of utility, however, we may remark that it can be made to mean either of two different things. In the first place, utility can be regarded as not only conceivable in quantitative terms, but also actually measurable. Or in the second place, it can be regarded as so measurable only in principle, but not in actual practice. The question, therefore, is which of the two possibilities does the cardinalist really visualise? It will be evident as we proceed that it is the former view which is essential to orthodox cardinalist theory while many cardinalists would probably wish to be content with no more than the latter.

If the cardinalist were to remain content merely with the assertion of quantifiability-in-principle, then apart probably from a few philosophical qualms, the ordinalist would find remarkably little to quarrel about on the operational plane. For surely so long as utility cannot be measured in practice, it cannot be represented except ordinally; and from that point onwards the cardinal and the ordinal theories share the same operational consequences.

What gives a real edge to the quantifiability concept, it would be admitted therefore, is the second assumption implied by Marshall, viz., that marginal utility, quantifiable in principle, is actually also measurable in terms of money. If we looked upon money (as we surely must), as the general purchasing power, then in a general sense there can be no objection to regarding it as command over alternative *welfare-yielding* situations. It might therefore apparently be argued that the amount of sacrifice in terms of money (i.e., in terms of command over welfare-yielding situations) which a person would make rather than go without a particular thing, is a measure of his welfare derived from it. The difficulty, however, with this apparently sensible conclusion, as is now widely realised, rests with a further assumption which is implied and which is itself far less defensible.

If money is supposed to provide the measuring rod of utility, then evidently, as with all measuring rods, its unit must be invariant: it must measure the same amount of utility in *all* circumstances. The first pound must mean the same to the individual as the hundredth or the millionth. Just as we can say of an area of land that the first acre is equal to any other, so we must be able to say of welfare measured in terms of money that the first pound's equivalent of welfare is the same as the hundredth or the millionth pound's equivalent. With this general observation we leave the assumption of constant marginal utility of money for the present, and turn to the second stage of the Marshallian argument. We shall, however, have to return to it in due course.

III

The hypothesis that marginal utility is measurable in terms of money establishes the *raison d'être* of (consumer) demand price. We are still, however, a step farther from the 'law of demand' which would envisage a demand curve sloping downwards to the right. We are enabled to take this remaining step towards the enunciation of the Marshallian demand theorem by means of a further assumption regarding marginal utility. This assumption is embodied in Marshall's *'law of satiable wants or diminishing utility'*. This 'law', which represented, in Marshall's view, 'a familiar and fundamental tendency of human nature,'[1] ensured that, 'the additional benefit which a person derives from a given increase of his stock of a thing, diminishes with every increase in the stock he already has.'[2]

Given the principle of diminishing marginal utility, and *other things remaining the same*, the law of demand is simply derived: a downward-sloping marginal-utility schedule, expressed in terms of money, is transformed into a downward-sloping demand schedule. The inverse price-demand relationship is deduced from the inverse relationship between marginal utility and the quantity in stock.

IV

In our view, the methodological objection to the cardinal utility theory in the Marshallian form can be on two grounds. In the first place, as we shall presently demonstrate, it can be argued that the Marshallian demand theorem cannot genuinely be derived from the marginal-utility hypothesis except in a one-commodity model, without contradicting the assumption of constant marginal utility of money. We shall argue, in other words, that the constancy of the marginal utility of money is incom-

---

[1] Marshall, *Principles*, Eighth Edition, p. 93.
[2] *Ibid*.

patible with a proof of the demand theorem in a situation where the consumer has more than a single good to spread his expenditure on. If we avoid this difficulty by giving up the assumption of constant marginal utility of money, then money can no longer provide the measuring rod, and we can no longer express the marginal utility of a commodity in units of money.

This if condition is void

If we cannot express marginal utility in terms of a common numeraire (which money is defined to be), the 'cardinality' of utility would be devoid of any operational significance. As we have already observed, if the cardinalist is forced to be confined to the mere assertion that utility is quantifiable in principle and is unable to retain the further assumption that it can be measured in terms of observables and in units of constant magnitude, then surely his utility theory becomes indistinguishable from the ordinal theory except perhaps, on a purely philosophical plane.

The objection that the demand theorem and the assumption of constant marginal utility of money are incompatible except in a single-good model, amounts to pointing out an infringement of our first and 'positive' condition for admissibility of a utility-hypothesis, 'that a meaningful and valid theorem can genuinely be derived from it.' If this objection is admitted then we should be justified in rejecting the cardinal-utility hypothesis without reference to the negative assertion (which also we shall be making) that a 'better' hypothesis (as defined by our *third* condition) is available, and should be chosen on grounds of 'economy'.

The 'negative' condition that there should be 'no

alternative hypothesis known which can enunciate a more general theorem on the same assumptions or the same theorem on fewer assumptions' would suggest, as we have already hinted, our second methodological objection to the cardinal-utility hypothesis. It can be argued that even if the derivation of the demand theorem could validly be made from the Marshallian hypothesis, it would still have to be rejected, because a 'better' hypothesis was available. As we shall see in due course, the Hicksian in-difference-preference hypothesis is based on fewer assump-tions than the cardinal-utility theory. And yet it is able to enunciate a *more general* demand theorem. In fact, we shall be arguing that the assumption of constant marginal utility of money obscured Marshall's insight into the truly *composite* character of the unduly simplified price-demand relationship.[1] The efficiency and precision with which the Hicks-Allen approach can distinguish between the 'in-come' and the 'substitution' effects of a price-change really leaves the cardinalist argument in a very poor state indeed.

We devote the rest of the present chapter, however, only

[1] We must not fail to acknowledge, however, the part Marshall played in emphasising the difficulty in formulating a 'universal' law of demand, though admittedly he did not see that it was his 'cardinalism' which was causing most of the trouble. It was entirely owing to his insistence that the implication of the Giffen case (introduced for the first time in *Principles*, Third Edition), which he made famous, was first realised.

It is interesting to note that this Giffen case (of a *positively* sloped de-mand curve), as Stigler's researches seem to indicate, may never have existed at all! (See G. J. Stigler, 'Notes on the History of the Giffen Paradox', *Journal of Political Economy*, April 1947.) That Marshall was able to read so much into what he himself called Giffen's 'hint' (see his letter quoted by Stigler) which eventually led to the correct non-Marshallian formulation of the demand theorem, is by itself a tribute to that great man.

to the consideration of our first objection to the Marshallian case. The other objection would be apparent only in course of our elaboration of the Slutsky-Hicks-Allen ordinal-utility theory which forms the subject-matter of the next chapter.

V

Let us consider the case of a consumer with a given income to spend on a number of commodities.[1] In the simplest form of the Marshallian argument, the utility derived by the consumer from any one of the commodities would be independent of that derived from any other. There would not be, in other words, either the relation of substitution or that of complementarity present between any two commodities. In a more complex form of the argument, both these relations may be implied. Of course, in the Marshallian analysis, circumscribed as it is by the famous *ceteris paribus* clause, we can do no more than hint at interrelation.

The equilibrium of the consumer with a given amount of money to spend on a number of commodities with given prices, would be determined by the well-known proportionality rule. The consumer would reach his equilibrium at a position in which he finds the marginal utility of each commodity proportional to its price. When marginal

---

[1] The demonstration that follows is mainly due to Hicks. Cf., J. R. Hicks, *A Revision of Demand Theory*, pp. 9–15. Hicks, however, as the reader would notice, arrives at a conclusion ('Cardinalism has eliminated itself': p. 15), which is substantially different from ours. The difference, we suggest, is probably due to the consideration weighing with Hicks that the contradiction brought out in the demonstration is less damaging to Marshall's demand theory than it is to his utility theory.

utility is assumed to be measurable in terms of money, the proportionality rule signifies that the marginal utility of a commodity under equilibrium conditions would be equal to its price multiplied by the marginal utility of money (which serves as the unit of utility measurement).

Let us suppose that we start with an equilibrium position in which the proportionality condition has been fulfilled; and also that the consumer under equilibrium purchases the quantity q_1 of a commodity X, at price p_1. The marginal utility of X, at this position, would therefore be equal to the product of p_1 and the unit of measurement, the marginal utility of money. Also, the total amount of money spent on X would be $p_1 . q_1$ at the point of equilibrium. Let us now imagine that the price of the commodity X has risen from p_1 to p_2. The marginal utility of X would now be found less than its price multiplied by the marginal utility of money (assuming, of course, that the latter has not changed). Since the marginal-utility curve is assumed to slope down to the right, the equilibrating adjustment would take the form of a fall in demand for X, so that its marginal utility rises and becomes equal once again to the product of the new price and the marginal utility of money. If the total amount spent on the new quantity of X, q_2 (say), at the new price p_2, happened to be exactly the same as the total amount spent on the old quantity at the old price, no further complication need ensue. The Marshallian theory, however, breaks down as soon as it is realised that this accidental equality would be only a minor possibility.

The new amount spent $(p_2 q_2)$ would be smaller or larger than the old amount $(p_1 q_1)$ depending on whether the marginal-utility curve of X (in the particular region) is elastic or inelastic. In the first case, the consumer would be left with more money to spend on the commodities other than X; in the second case he would be left with less, given of course, that in both cases his total available income is fixed. Whether the new amount spent on X is smaller or larger than the old amount, a fresh complication in the attainment of the equilibrium position is introduced so long as the two amounts are *different*. As soon as a difference between the two amounts is visualised, evidently a further adjustment of the consumer's expenditure on commodities *other than X* is called for. In Marshallian terms this further adjustment can take only one form: the revision of the unit of utility measurement, i.e., the marginal utility of money.

Except in a strictly one-commodity world, therefore, the assumption of a constant marginal utility of money would be incompatible with the Marshallian demand theorem. Without the assumption of an invariant unit of measurement, the assertion of measurability of utility would be entirely meaningless. The necessity and the possibility of a revision of the unit of utility measurement, following every change in price, had been assumed away in the Marshallian theory under cover of the 'other things remaining the same' clause. Needless to add that the recognition of this necessity destroys the usefulness, as well as the validity of the 'measurability-in-fact' part of the cardinal hypothesis.

We end up, therefore, with a simple and straightforward case against the cardinal-utility hypothesis: that it must give up the vital assumption of an *invariant* and *observable* unit of utility measurement, as soon as a certain theorem (the law of demand) derived from it, is sought to be adjusted to conditions outside a single-commodity world.

This, in our opinion, constitutes a sufficient infringement of the first (and 'positive') condition of admissibility for an 'introspective' hypothesis; which warrants the conclusion that the case for maintaining the *orthodox* cardinalist position in utility theory in any *operationally significant sense*, does not exist.

CHAPTER VI

The Introspective Ordinalist

I

Our comment in the preceding chapter on the introspective method in economic science has implied a point which, though trivial, needs to be made explicit at this stage, if only to avoid a possible misunderstanding about it. It is merely this, that the method has been defined by us as the procedure of admitting a hypothesis which is not immediately observable, but which seeks to *explain observable facts*. An 'introspective' hypothesis, though not itself capable of being refuted or verified at the level of actual observation is still admissible if (and only if) it can be shown to have observable consequences. An admissible introspective hypothesis is, therefore, a procedural abstraction which aims at simplifying our understanding of *observed* data.

The point which we wish to make explicit now is twofold. In the first place, it must be understood that the method of 'introspection', *in our sense*, is *not* a method of *formulating* hypotheses about facts.[1] In the second place,

---

[1] Though we are quite unable to share Mr. Little's low opinion of the place of methodology in economics, we are completely at one with him on the point that, 'there is no technique for forming good hypotheses which can be taught.' But whether this does not provide a plausible argument in favour of trying to evolve a 'technique for *testing* hypotheses which can be taught', is a different matter. Methodology, it is true, is as Little says, 'unlikely to help students reach new theories of their own.' It would

the method, again in our sense, *has no place for introspection as a means of testing hypotheses about facts*.

The method of introspection, as we have tried to explain, consists of testing and admitting a given hypothesis (arrived at, anyhow, through introspection), which is not itself falsifiable, but which has falsifiable consequences. And the testing of a given hypothesis consists of finding out how far (*a*) it is useful in the explanation of its falsifiable consequences; and (*b*) how far its falsifiable consequences are found to be valid (i.e., not falsified). The method of introspection, by our definition, is interpersonally invariant. With these additional comments on our methodological classification, we now return to our subject-matter.

II

We are concerned in the present chapter with the Hicks-Allen hypothesis in utility theory. The basic methodological approach here is the same as in the Marshallian marginal-utility hypothesis: it is, that is to say, mainly introspective.[1]

Ordinal-utility theory, as we have already observed, enjoys an initial advantage over its rival which certainly makes it, at least *prima facie*, the more attractive. An ordi-

---

however, serve its purpose rather well if it helps students to discard some theories of their professors. (See I. M. D. Little, *A Critique of Welfare Economics*, Second Edition, p. 1.)

[1] This remains so in spite of Professor Hicks' recent *Revision of Demand Theory*. If, by the 'econometric approach' (pp. 1–7, loc. cit.) to which he now feels so enormously attracted, he really means that every category in his system must have an econometric *definition*, then it is clearly inconsistent with his 'indifference' hypothesis; and if, he merely means that every admissible category must *eventually* refer to facts, then the 'new' approach is indistinguishable from his earlier (introspective) method!

nal theory does not *have to* assume independent, absolute identifiability of welfare while orthodox cardinalism is tied to that assumption from the start. This methodological advantage would no doubt be rather overwhelming once the ordinal-utility hypothesis can be made to stand on its own: if, that is to say, it can explain at least as much as the cardinal theory does.

If the derivation of the demand theorem is our test, as we had intended it to be, then evidently the requirement is that the ordinal theory must establish (or disprove or otherwise clarify) the inverse relation alleged to exist between price and demand without making any more assumptions than those implied in the cardinal theory. We shall, of course, disregard for the time being, as prudence would certainly suggest, the otherwise vital consideration that we have already had to reject the orthodox cardinal hypothesis on its own ground!

It will be our contention, if we may anticipate our argument in the following sections, (a) that the Hicks-Allen type of ordinal-utility theory satisfies the above requirement; (b) that moreover, the ordinal theory succeeds in stating the relationship between a given change in the price of a commodity and its demand in a *composite* form, distinguishing between the 'income' and the 'substitution' effects, which fills in a genuine gap in the Marshallian statement of the 'law of demand'; (c) that the traces of 'cardinalist' thinking, which are undoubtedly present in the usual indifference-preference analysis, do not constitute its essential elements; and finally (d) that the abandonment of the *continuous* indifference curves in the revised 'logical' statement of the Hicksian theory[1] frees it completely from the remnants of cardinalism.

The following is a brief account of the familiar Hicks-Allen argument in terms of the consumer-indifference curves.

It is assumed that while the consumer may be unable to assess any individual welfare positions, say, A or B, independently and in quantitative terms, he is nevertheless able to *compare* between A and B to know whether he prefers one to the other or is indifferent between the two. It is further assumed that (*a*) *both* preference and indifference relations are *transitive*, so that if the individual prefers A to B and B to C, he is said to prefer A to C; similarly if he is indifferent between A and B, and also between B and C, he is said to be indifferent between A and C; and (*b*) the consumer is rational in the sense that he prefers more of a commodity to less.

The so-called indifference curves in the ordinal theory are usually derived through a process of systematic substitution. An initial position is visualised for the consumer where he starts with given stocks of different commodities. It is then argued that if the consumer is now deprived continuously of one commodity, he can be offered, at every stage, suitable increments in other commodities so as every time to compensate fully for his loss. The result, no doubt, gives a number of situations arranged in the descending order of his stock in one commodity and an

[1] Cf. J. R. Hicks, *A Revision of Demand Theory*, Chapter III, 'The Preference Hypothesis', and Chapter IV, 'The Logic of Order.' See, specially, pp. 18–19.

ascending order of his stock in some other. In every situation the consumer finds that compared to the preceding one, he has a compensating gain in one direction to offset his loss in another. The consumer is defined to be in a state of 'indifference' between any two such situations.

To follow the ordinalist argument a little further, let us suppose that a series of situations, say, B, C, D, E, etc. have been derived systematically as described above, starting from an initial position of A. The consumer is, therefore, by definition in a state of indifference between A and B; B and C; C and D; and D and E. This relation of indifference, it has to be emphasised, is conceptually a *positive* relation: it does not merely signify that the consumer cannot choose between the two situations concerned; it also means that the consumer can, in principle, *name* one such situation as the *price* for another.

The relation of ordinal indifference is the exact equivalent of the relation of 'equality' in the cardinal sense. Thus the axiom of transitivity of ordinal indifference emerges automatically and is no more subject to dispute than is the axiom of transitivity of numerical equality. A moment's reflection would also show that the relation of ordinal indifference is necessarily non-directional. If, as in our illustration, A, B, C, D and E, being derived in that order through systematic substitution of one commodity by another, show that there exists a relation of indifference between A and B, B and C, etc., then following the axiom of transitivity there exists a relation of indifference between *any* pair of the above situations. All such situations, that is to say, belong (in a two-commodity world) to the same indifference curve of the consumer.

The convenience of deriving indifference curves (or surfaces) through the above mentioned process of *continuous* and orderly substitution of one commodity by another, however, makes it all the more necessary for us to add a warning: one must not be tempted to try to find a logical necessity in the *order* of the situations such as *A*, *B*, *C*, *D*, etc. *C*, for example, could as well have been derived from *A*, or *D*, say, as from *B*.

It has probably been a little unwise on the part of the ordinalist (historically speaking) to visualise *A*, *B*, *C*, etc. in *order*, and *then* to postulate transitivity in the case of *indifference* relations, though the procedure would be perfectly justifiable in the case of *preference* relations. There is no order, no direction, and no necessity of sequence in a number of situations, each one of which is defined to be a full substitute for another. Any pair of situations linked by the relation of ordinal indifference are linked *directly* to each other (as situations linked by the relation of cardinal 'equality' would be) as shown in Diagram 3 below. This link does not depend on the consumer's ability to proceed through (even mentally) situations arranged only in a given order, such as, say, a descending order of his stock of one commodity and, therefore, an ascending order of his stock of another. That the situations dealt with for the purpose of exposition have not only been arranged in such order but also actually been conceived to belong to a *continuous* curve has undoubtedly made ordinal theory attractive to the students of mathematics. But unfortunately, it has not contributed to the understanding of the logic of ordering. In Diagram 2 below, we have the usual indifference curve. We can see at a glance that its logical

F

properties are less apparent than those of the network in Diagram 3. Once we realise this, however, the grounds for abandoning the indifference curve at least for expository purposes seem to us to be highly debatable. With the simple reservation that we do not read into a geometrical construction more than the logic it is meant to demonstrate would permit, we shall find it useful, in spite of the recent misgivings of Hicks on the question,[1] to have the indifference curves after all.

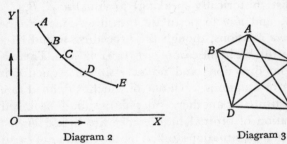

Diagram 2   Diagram 3

We have, then, been able to make two rather important points about the nature of ordinal indifference. In the first place, indifference is established to be a *strong* relation, which implies that if the consumer is indifferent between two situations, he can name one as *compensation* for the loss of the other. This is a very different proposition from the mere statement of a weak indifference relation, implying only that the consumer cannot choose between the two situations concerned.[2]

[1] *A Revision of Demand Theory*, loc. cit.

[2] The idea of indifference as based on the principle of compensation gives it a positive ('strong') content. The usual practice of describing an ordering which consists only of preference relations as 'strong' and one which takes into account both preference and indifference relations as 'weak', is, therefore, somewhat deceptive in utility theory; it should, in our opinion, best be avoided.

In the second place, it follows from the definition of 'strong' indifference that *compensation* (and *not approximation*)[1] is its conceptual basis. The method of continuous substitution for obtaining the indifference curves is useful, but not necessary. Which also goes to show that arguments, commonly levelled against the 'continuity' of indifference curves, are not arguments against the concept of *compensated-indifference* which constitutes the basic hypothesis of the Hicks-Allen utility theory.

With these two important reservations in mind, we may now turn to the familiar geometrical device for a demonstration of the crucial price-demand relationship.

In the following diagram the consumer is represented as facing a two-commodity market. The two commodities in question are X and Y. We may conveniently assume that X is a single commodity, and Y represents all the other commodities, i.e., money. The price ratio between X and Y is given; so is the consumer's income, which is OA in terms of money, and given the price ratio, OB in terms of X. The points on any one indifference curve bear relations of strong indifference to one another. From the assumption of preference-transitivity and rationality it follows that the farther the consumer moves to the right, the higher the level of satisfaction he reaches. The indifference curves fall to the right, and assuming that the consumer is in equilibrium (at some combination of X and Y), are convex to the origin.

---

[1] An idea of 'indifference' based on the principle of approximation would not be non-directional and transitive. If, for example, A is only approximately equivalent to B, and B approximately equivalent to C, then it no longer follows that A would be equivalent to C. The concept of intransitive indifference (which is due to Armstrong), is quite consistent with Hicksian transitive indifference. See Chapter IX below.

Given the price ratio, and his income, the best that the consumer can do is evidently to choose P, on the indifference curve I. At this point the slope of I, which we may define (following Hicks) as the marginal rate of substitution of X for Y, must be equal to the price ratio, which is the slope of AB.

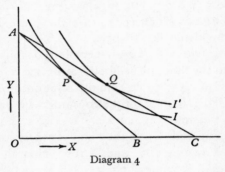

Diagram 4

If we compare the consumer-equilibrium conditions of the ordinal theory with those of the Marshallian version, the following propositions would be evident: (i) that the equality of the marginal rate of substitution and the price ratio is the ordinal equivalent of the condition that marginal utilities are proportional to prices; (ii) that the convexity of indifference curves (ensuring diminishing marginal rate of substitution) is equivalent to assuming diminishing marginal utility; and (iii) that the assumption of constant marginal utility of money, i.e., of Y in our illustration, is unnecessary in ordinal theory and has no ordinal counterpart.

We may also point out that *if* marginal utilities were measurable in principle, then their ratios (which would be the marginal rates of substitution) would be measurable in practice.[1] If, however, we do not assume that marginal utilities are measurable even in principle, we can still have the marginal rates of substitution: which is another distinct advantage of the ordinal formulation.

To come back to our demonstration, let us suppose that the price of X falls and that the same income can now buy OC of X. The new equilibrium position would be Q. Barring the Giffen case (which does not have the shapes of the indifference curves as shown), to which we shall return in the following section, Q would lie to the right of P. Thus with a fall in the price of X, its demand will increase, unless the shapes of the indifference curves are such as to place Q behind P, in which case the law of demand will not hold.

When we remember that the Marshallian theory states the law of demand without being able to account for the Giffen paradox, it would be evident that the ordinal theory even at this stage, has satisfied the minimum requirement for its admissibility: it has enunciated the demand theorem at least as fully as (or rather, not less completely than) the cardinal theory and has done so on *fewer* assumptions.

Having established that the ordinal theory is at least as efficient as the cardinal,[2] we shall now proceed to demon-

---

[1] Cf., for example, Hicks, *A Revision of Demand Theory*, p. 12 ('All that we shall be able to measure is what the ordinal theory grants to be measurable — namely, the ratio of the marginal utility of one commodity to the marginal utility of another'). See, however, our comment on this statement by Hicks in Section V below.

[2] Even at this stage the ordinalist argument is sounder. It can precisely point out that the 'trouble' in the Giffen case lies in the shapes of the indifference curves, that is, in the nature of the preference relationship between the two commodities concerned. Marshallian analysis, being forced to take one good at a time, is unable to visualise the nature of 'inferior' goods.

strate that the indifference-preference analysis is able to state a more general theorem than Marshall's 'law of demand'.

IV

As we have seen above, to go back to Diagram 4, the fall in the price of X enables the consumer to shift from I to I', i.e., from a lower to a higher level of welfare. Similarly, a rise in the price of X would force the consumer down to a lower indifference curve, and therefore, a lower level of welfare. In other words, the fall (rise) in the price of X, does to the consumer exactly what a rise (fall) in income would have done to him. The consumer, therefore, may be represented as reaching the higher (lower) level of welfare through a gain (loss) in income rather than a fall (rise) in price. The welfare consequences, that is to say, of a change in price, can be translated into those of a change in income.

The equivalence of a given change in price to a suitable change in income is a major discovery of ordinal-utility analysis. That this fundamental relation necessarily remains obscure in the cardinal single-good model and when assuming constant marginal utility of money, while it emerges clearly and immediately in a related-goods model *without* the cardinalist assumption, leaves very little doubt indeed as to the outcome of the cardinal-ordinal controversy.

As soon as we comprehend the effect of a price change on the level of welfare, the relationship between price and demand assumes a composite character. A fall in price raises the consumer's level of welfare by (*a*) making it *possible* for him to buy more of *all* commodities; and (*b*) making it *profitable* for him to buy more of the commodity which has grown cheaper, and *less* of all other commodities.

The first effect can be compared, as we have seen above, to that of a rise in income. It would be evident that whether the consumer would actually take advantage of the favourable price-income situation to buy more of *all* commodities depends on a further consideration. If the consumer's demand for a particular commodity is positively income-elastic, then and only then would he be induced to buy more of it when his income alone rises. Therefore, the 'income-effect' of a fall in price depends on whether the income-elasticity of demand for the other goods (as well as that of demand for the good of which the price has fallen) is positive or negative. In the case of 'inferior' goods the income-elasticity is (defined to be) negative.

While the 'income-effect' depends on whether the commodity in question is a normal or an inferior good, the 'substitution-effect' which induces the consumer to buy more of the cheaper good is universally present. The two effects taken together actually determine the observed price-demand relationship.

For normal goods, both the income- and the substitution-effects naturally act in the same direction. The income-effect ensures, when the price of a good has fallen, that the consumer buys more of it because he can now afford to do so; the substitution-effect ensures that he buys more of it because it has now become profitable to replace the other goods (which have become marginally, relatively more expensive) by it. This, therefore, accounts for the validity of the demand theorem in 'normal' circumstances.

When a commodity is considered by the consumer to be an 'inferior' good, he tries to get out of it as soon as he can afford to. So in the case of an inferior good the income-effect runs counter to the substitution-effect. But so long as the commodity in question does not occupy too large a place in the consumer's budget, the income-effect may not be overwhelming for the substitution-effect. In such circumstances the net effect on the demand for a commodity which has become cheaper, would still be positive. This accounts for the large number of 'inferior' goods for which also the law of demand holds as good as for normal goods.

Apart from 'normal' goods and those 'inferior' goods for which the income-effect of a change in price would be smaller in magnitude than the substitution-effect, there may still remain inferior goods for which the income-effect would be *larger* than the substitution-effect. To this small (perhaps non-existent) class of goods belongs the famous Giffen-bread, for which the law of demand does not hold.

Thus the ordinal-utility theory enables us to enunciate the general theorem of demand in the following composite form, to which the Marshallian 'law' constitutes a special case:

(a) The demand for a commodity varies inversely with price when the income-elasticity of demand for that commodity is *nil or positive*;

(b) The demand for a commodity varies inversely with price when the income-effect of a change in price is *smaller* than the substitution-effect;

(c) The demand for a commodity varies directly with price when the income-elasticity of demand for that commodity is *negative*, *and* the income-effect of a change in price is *larger* than the substitution effect.

When either the first or the second condition is fulfilled, the Marshallian 'law of demand' holds. When neither condition is satisfied, we get the Giffen case of a positively sloping demand curve.

v

Finally, we must dispose of a small but somewhat troublesome methodological question which remains to be settled. It is possible to argue, as would be evident from what follows, that the concept of 'indifference' in Hicksian theory is not entirely free from an essentially cardinal element. Now, if this argument were valid, then at one stroke the cardinalist (though not the Marshallian) case could be rehabilitated. It is our contention below that though there are traces of cardinalist thinking in the Hicksian theory, these do not constitute its essential part, and that the abandonment of the 'continuous' indifference curves (in the recent 'revision' of demand theory) marks for Hicks a definite break with his cardinalist preconceptions.

The argument that the relation of indifference implies a cardinal element follows from quite a simple consideration. The consumer can visualise an indifference relation, it is argued, because he is assumed to be able to see what constitutes his compensation for a marginal loss in any particular direction. He can visualise, in other words, the marginal rate of substitution of one commodity for another. Now, this rate has been described (by Hicks himself, amongst others), as the ratio of two marginal utilities. Again and again, the theme recurs in Hicksian analysis that, 'all that we shall be able to measure is what the ordinal theory grants to be measurable — namely the ratio of the marginal utility of one commodity to the marginal utility of another.'[1] But, surely a ratio cannot be measured unless the two marginal utilities concerned are at least quantifiable in principle? One cannot talk of a fraction with two non-quantifiable entities as the numerator and the denominator! Therefore, it may be contended that the idea of indifference in Hicksian terms essentially involves an admission that utility is quantifiable in principle.

It is precisely this anomaly which we have tried to avoid in our own statement of the indifference-preference theory. And it is our contention that we have succeeded in demonstrating (a) that a *continuous* derivation of the indifference curve involving the use of marginal rates of substitution in an essential way is not only unnecessary, but also somewhat misleading, since it is likely to obscure the 'strong' assumption implied in the definition of indifference; (b) that the marginal rate of substitution in any case can be so defined as to make its meaning independent of the meaning of marginal utility: *if* marginal utilities are taken to be quantifiable, then their ratios certainly give the marginal rates of substitution; but if not, the marginal rate of substitution can still be derived as a meaningful concept from the logic of the compensation-principle; and (c) that with these two important qualifications in mind, it is

[1] Cf. *A Revision of Demand Theory*, p. 12.

nevertheless convenient to use the simple geometrical device of indifference curves for a demonstration of the demand theorem.

In a strictly logical presentation of the indifference-preference hypothesis, as Hicks now contends,[1] the 'continuous' indifference curves should best be disregarded as an analytical tool of any promise whatsoever. And an analysis in terms of simple verbal logic does help Hicksian theory remove the last of its cardinalist preconceptions: the assumption of continuity in the individual's preference field. But, as we have tried to emphasise above, *if* (and only if) the logical implications are explicitly stated and we are not prepared to be carried away by the elegance of infinitesimal calculi, the geometrical presentation of the indifference analysis may continue to be used as an important aid to understanding all but the most complicated problems in consumer-behaviour theory.

[1] *Ibid.*, pp. 16–35.

CHAPTER VII

The Behaviourist Ordinalist

I

In Marshallian and Hicksian utility theories we came upon the application of what we had defined as the 'introspective' method in economics. We shall now turn to an examination of some of the results obtained through the alternative method which is the hall-mark of the ordinal-utility theory of Samuelson on the one hand, and the cardinal-utility theory of the followers of Morgenstern and von Neumann on the other. We had described this other method in so far as it applied to utility theory as 'behaviourist'. A further consideration of the general nature of the behaviourist method is perhaps necessary before we can proceed to assess the specific results of its application to our problem of measurability of utility.

We may remember that the introspective method (a) aimed at *understanding* and not merely *describing* observed phenomena by means of formulating (b) general propositions which are *not observable by themselves*, but (c) which nevertheless have observable *consequences*. The behaviourist would argue that 'understanding' or 'explanation' of observed phenomena except in the sense of precise and accurate description can have no operational meaning, and therefore, no role in scientific investigation. The universe of scientific knowledge, according to the behaviourist, must consist entirely of refutable *data*; whatever lie beyond the known universe of scientific knowledge, must be either further (undiscovered) refutable data, or entities devoid of operational significance, and therefore, beyond the scope and method of science.

The introspectionist and the behaviourist would both agree that the meaningfulness of a hypothesis depends on its refutability. Their disagreement turns on the question of the meaning of refutability of a hypothesis. As we had also remarked on an earlier occasion, what constitutes refutation is necessarily a question of procedure.[1] While refutability in the behaviourist procedure amounts to direct empiric falsifiability of the hypothesis in question, in the introspective procedure it implies falsifiability of only the consequences of the hypothesis.

The universe of knowledge for the introspectionist, therefore, would consist of two types of entities: (*a*) refutable *data*; and (*b*) *explanatory* hypotheses which are not observable in data form, but which have observable consequences. We have already observed that the second type of entities would be excluded from the behaviourist meaning of scientific knowledge.

One final distinction between the two methods which seems to have an immediate bearing on our present problem: the meaning of a behaviourist hypothesis is exactly the *same* as the meaning of the theorem or theorems it enunciates, and its role is purely descriptive. But the meaning of a genuinely introspective hypothesis *must be different* from meaning of the theorem or theorems it enunciates: for its role is mainly explanatory.

[1] See Chapter II, pp. 24–27 above.

Thus the behaviourist method only admits falsifiable general propositions (such as, say, 'the conditions of equilibrium are equivalent to the maximisation of some magnitude'), which would be 'general' simply in the sense of being a *summary* of falsifiable particular propositions (such as, 'the conditions of consumer-equilibrium are equivalent to the maximisation of utility'). The introspective method, in contrast, would admit *non-instantial* general propositions (such as, say, the 'law of satiable wants'), of which only particular instances (such as the 'law of demand') can be stated in observable, i.e., falsifiable form.[1]

It follows that no *a priori* grounds for choosing between the two methods can be offered which would be acceptable irrespective of personal (philosophical, etc.) inclinations. Behaviourism certainly has the great advantage of treading only on observed ground: it cannot go wrong. But whether it goes far enough is the question. It may also be claimed for the method of introspection that operationally, it can get all the results which are obtained by the alternative method, *and* it presumes to go farther: it not only states, but also explains its theorems.

An explanation also cannot go wrong, provided that (*a*) the theorem it claims to explain, logically follows from it; and (*b*) it is not observed to be a false theorem. But any explanation can certainly be refuted *eventually*: either because one of its observable consequences comes to be falsified, or simply because a more 'economical' explanation is discovered. Since every genuine explanation (as dis-

[1] The reader will, perhaps, notice that the first set of theorems is due to Samuelson (*Foundations of Economic Analysis*) and the second set to Marshall.

tinguished from a merely operational summary) of facts
waits to be discarded in time in favour of a more general
explanation, the method of introspection has a true open
end. And that really constitutes, according to one's taste,
its strength or its weakness.

II

The rest of the chapter is devoted to an examination of
the behaviourist ordinal-utility theory of Samuelson. The
behaviourist cardinalists are dealt with in the next chapter.

The main distinguishing feature of Samuelson's theory
in so far as it concerns the problem of welfare measurability is the hypothesis of 'strong' ordering. It is our contention below that an implicit assumption in Samuelson's
theory rules out the possibility of 'weak' ordering, i.e., the
possibility of 'indifference' being an operationally significant concept. This, as we shall see, is the familiar assumption of 'two-term consistency' which also lies at the basis
of Hicksian indifference-preference analysis.[1]

It will readily be realised, perhaps, that the relations of
'preference' and 'indifference' as applied to welfare
situations would be admissible in behaviourist theory only
if these can be defined in an operationally meaningful way.
So far as 'preference' is concerned, the behaviourist requirement does not present any particularly difficult problem. It may be remembered how the axiom of Revealed
Preference is introduced in the behaviourist procedure of
welfare identification.[2] As we have already remarked, it is
this axiom which provides the necessary operational link

[1] See, *A Revision of Demand Theory*, p. 26.
[2] Cf. Chapter II, Section V above; also Appendix below.

between observed choice-behaviour and the behaviourist's welfare-conclusions. We have also demonstrated how this vital link between behaviourist economics and welfare theory tends to break down in conditions under which the use of strategy is not ruled out. In the more usual perfect-competition models, however, the operational meaningfulness of the relation of 'preference' defined in a welfare sense is quite admissible.

What is really difficult to be conceived of operationally is the relation of 'indifference'. It is obvious that no single act on the part of the consumer in terms of choice can prove his indifference between two situations. If we are disinclined to admit a statement about the measurement of welfare unless it can be related to a single specific and demonstrable act, then surely the relation of 'indifference' must be judged a meaningless concept for our purpose? Given the particular resolution as to the admissibility of a preference hypothesis, the rejection of 'indifference' in Samuelson's theory is, therefore, not a matter of convenience, but dictated by the requirements of his methodology.

And yet, it would be evident on a little reflection that the rejection of the relation of 'indifference' on operational grounds does involve an assumption, which is in addition to the basic behaviourist resolution. This assumption may be simply stated thus: 'no two observations of choice-behaviour are made which provide conflicting evidence to the individual's preference.' In other words, if the individual is found to have chosen A, say, rather than B in a particular instance, then he cannot (consistently) choose B rather than A in any other instance. Thus the consistency of the individual is related to his each single act of choice. This is what Hicks has called his 'two-term consistency'.[1]

It is easy to see that a wider operational meaning to the concept of the individual's consistency can possibly be given. Thus, we could say, for example, that the individual shows a consistent preference for A over B, if (a) he chooses A rather than B more frequently than he chooses B rather than A, over a given number of observations; and (b) he does not choose B rather than A more frequently than he chooses A rather than B when the same or a larger number of observations are made again. In other words, consistency can be defined in a statistical sense, given an additional procedural resolution as to an adequate sample-size.

As soon as this possibility emerges, the rejection of 'indifference' on behaviourist grounds alone no longer appears to be certain. For it may now be held that the individual is defined to be indifferent between two situations A and B, if a definite preference for either does not emerge from a sufficiently large number of observations. What constitutes a sufficiently large number in a particular case is, as we have remarked, a procedural question which cannot be answered on a purely *a priori* basis.

Thus, only because Samuelson implicitly confines two-term consistency to *single* acts of choice that the indifference-relation is methodologically inadmissible to his theory. The alternative procedure of statistical definitions of 'preference' and 'indifference' is equally open to the behaviourist method, as, of course, would be only too evident when we come to consider the experimental-cardinalist argument in the next chapter.

[1] *A Revision of Demand Theory*, loc. cit.

It should be realised that a consistency assumption is necessarily implied in every type of welfare theory. But we are not really troubled by it until and unless we are faced with the operationalist's dilemma: should we sacrifice the concept of indifference? Or, should we rather sacrifice the economy of drawing welfare conclusions from the observation of single acts of choice? And that question, for our purpose, resolves into another: can we obtain the same results from a purely strongly-ordered set of relations as we do from a weakly-ordered set? This, of course, leaves on one side the other obvious questions: (a) are conclusions from the observation of single acts of choice *valid*? and (b) is the 'statistical' method of interpreting the individual's preferences and indifferences similarly permissible? To each of the last two questions we should be able to provide at some stage at least a tentative answer. But for the rest of this chapter we shall merely grant an answer in the affirmative to '(a)' and leave '(b)' out as being not immediately relevant to our present consideration.[1]

Granting the single-act-revealed-preference assumption for the time being, we may now return once again to the task of enunciating the demand theorem, and check the efficiency of the Samuelsonian 'strong-ordering' hypothesis against that familiar and well-trusted test.

III

The behaviourist-ordinal demand theorem (in principle) can be an advance upon the Marshallian version only in a negative sense. As would be evident from what follows, its applicability is not more general than that of

[1] Cf. Chapter VIII, Section III below.

Marshall's 'law of demand': unlike the Hicksian theorem it does not aim to include the Giffen case. It only makes explicit an operationally meaningful condition (positive income-elasticity of demand), from which the theorem of inverse price-demand relationship is deduced by logical implication.

It will be our contention that the behaviourist ordinal theory is so circumscribed by its methodological procedure (of having to reject a hypothesis which is not *directly* testable, notwithstanding its operational consequences), that (a) it is unable to enunciate the demand theorem when the income-elasticity of demand is zero, or is negative but the income effect less than the substitution effect; and (b) it is unable to expand the demand theorem to allow for the case in which the income-elasticity of demand is negative *and* the income effect larger than the substitution-effect. To be more precise, it will be our contention that the behaviourist method is unable to replace (or admit) the substitution effect *which is the operational consequence* of the non-observable indifference hypothesis. Which would lead us to the (probably) unexpected but unavoidable conclusion that the Hicksian introspectionist theory has greater operational significance than the Samuelson-type behaviourist theory.

We may begin by recounting a demonstration of Samuelson's elegant 'Fundamental Theorem of Consumption Theory',[1] which states that 'any good (simple or composite) that is known always to increase in demand

---

[1] P. A. Samuelson, 'Consumption Theorems in Terms of Overcompensation rather than Indifference Comparisons', *Economica*, February 1953. The diagrammatic representation of the argument is ours.

when money income alone rises must definitely shrink in demand when its price alone rises'. Thus a positive income-elasticity of demand is advanced as a necessary qualification to the Marshallian inverse-price-demand principle.

To prove this theorem, let us suppose that the consumer devotes his entire income to the purchase of only two commodities, X and Y as shown on Diagram 5 below.

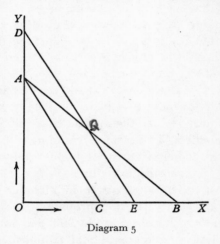

Diagram 5

Let the original price-income situation be represented by AB, and suppose further that the consumer is observed to have chosen the combination of X and Y represented by the point Q on AB. We may say that Q is 'revealed' to have been preferred to all other combinations of X and Y which were available to the consumer in the given price-income situation, i.e., to all points included within the area OAB. It is now our object to deduce the effect of a rise in the price of X on the consumer's demand for it, assuming that the consumer's demand varies directly with his income.

Suppose that the price of X rises and AC now represents the new price-income situation. Evidently, Q is no longer within the reach of the consumer and he must reduce the consumption of either X or Y or both. Let us, however, grant the consumer an extra money-income so that he can buy the same amount of everything at the higher price of X. The price-income situation, allowing for the extra money income (the cost-difference, as Hicks would have it), would be represented by DE (which would be parallel to AC) on which the point Q must also lie.

It would be evident that the consumer would not choose in the new situation a point below Q on DE, for the simple reason that Q has been revealed to have been preferred to any such point in the original price-income situation (all such points being contained within the area OAB). In other words, the consumer cannot now choose a combination which would give him a larger amount of X. Therefore, given the cost difference, the consumer will have either the same or a smaller amount of X. Let us now see what happens if the extra money allowance is withdrawn.

If the consumer can only have (to be consistent) either the same or a smaller amount of X *with* the money grant, he can only have a smaller amount of X *without* it, provided, of course, that his demand for X is known always to shrink with a fall in income. Thus granting a positive income-elasticity of demand, the inverse price-demand relationship is established so far as a *rise* in price is concerned. That the same relationship holds also for a fall in price would be evident from Diagram 6 below.

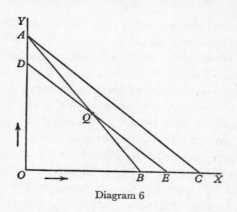

Diagram 6

Let us suppose that *AB* represents, as before, the consumer's original price-income situation and *Q* his preferred combination of *X* and *Y* in that situation. Suppose now that the price of *X* has fallen and that the new price-income line is *AC*.

Let us now follow our previous procedure (in reverse) and take away an amount of money from the consumer so that he is left with exactly enough to have *Q* in the new situation. The price-income line, allowing for the cost-difference taken from the consumer, passes through *Q* and is *DE* on the diagram. Once again, the consumer cannot choose (without being found inconsistent, that is) any point *above* *Q* on *DE*, since all such points were available to him in the original situation and, therefore, revealed to have been worse than *Q*, the chosen point. Which means that the consumer must choose either *Q* again, or a point farther down on *DE*. In other words, he must choose either the same amount of *X*, or more.

In either case, if we now hand him back the amount of the cost-difference originally taken away from him, he will clearly have *more* of *X* than he did at *Q*, provided, as before, that his demand for *X* moves in the same direction as his income.

The two demonstrations above together prove the theorem that any good which is known always to increase (decrease) in demand when money income alone rises (falls), must definitely shrink (expand) in demand when its price alone rises (falls).

The Samuelsonian demand theorem proceeds, therefore, from a single operationally refutable proposition: that the demand for a commodity changes in the same direction as that of a change in the income of the consumer. Since a general demand theorem in any case can be only directional and not quantitative, the operational significance of the Samuelson theorem is exactly the same as that of the case in which, in terms of the Hicksian theory, the substitution effect has been reinforced by the income-effect of a price change. On operational grounds, therefore, there should be nothing to choose between the behaviourist theorem and that part of the Hicksian theorem which takes into account a positive income-effect.

And yet, the behaviourist formulation seems to us to be profoundly dissatisfying on non-operational grounds alone. Granting for a moment that the substitution effect *cannot* be distinguished from the income effect on the plane of observation (which, as we shall be arguing presently, is not always true), questioning its meaningfulness is still an unnecessary scruple. We had observed on an earlier occasion, it may be remembered, that in all forms of welfare theory, indeed in *any* integral view of human activity, we have to *assume* that the individual can always compare his ends. If this axiom is not granted, the whole of welfare economics falls to the ground. And if the axiom *is* granted, then the idea of remaining on the same level of welfare while sacrificing something of one commodity for something else of another, will emerge automatically. Surely, it is the tacit assumption of comparability — the assumption that after all, one attaches the same kind of meaning to welfare perceptions from different sources — which makes it seem profitable that the commodity which becomes cheaper should increasingly be used to replace others which remain relatively dearer? That in fact, one might sometimes want to behave otherwise requires the special argument of exceptional circumstances, such as the consideration of an overwhelming and negative income-elasticity of demand would provide.

Unless the operationalist is prepared to discard the axiom of comparability between ends (which, incidentally, would take away most of the 'sense' from his 'meaningful' propositions), he is implicitly committed to the concept of substitution. It does not add, or so it seems to us, to the strength of the operationalist's position, if he scrupled to concede the possibility of substitution between situations while he did not scruple to concede their mutual comparability.

Nevertheless, as we have observed above, so long as the demand theorem is only directional, the operational effect of positive income-elasticity of demand and that of substitution reinforced by positive income-elasticity will be exactly the same. So long as the income-effect (in Hicksian terminology) is positive, the presence of the substitution-effect has no additional observable consequence. And for the same reason, the two cases, (a) in which the substitution effect is stronger than a negative income effect, and (b) in which the substitution effect is weaker than a negative income effect, have only one and the same operational consequence: that given a negative income-elasticity of demand, the change in demand owing to a change in price is *indeterminate*. In other words, that the behaviourist theory (i) cannot enunciate the demand theory when the substitution effect is stronger than a negative income effect, and (ii) cannot enunciate the Giffen case when the substitution effect is weaker than a negative income effect, is a defect of that theory *from the introspectionist point of view only*, because in either case the substitution effect cannot be isolated on the plane of observation.

But there *can* exist a case in which the operational significance of substitution will be distinct. It is the case in which the income-elasticity of demand is nil. The behaviourist method, being unable to recognise the substitution effect, cannot enunciate a demand theorem for this case. The introspectionist method can do so unequivocally, thus:

> 'Any good which is known always to remain unaffected in demand when money-income alone rises (falls), must definitely shrink (expand) in demand when its price alone rises (falls).'

As formulated, the demand theorem for zero-elasticity

of demand with respect to income, is a directly testable proposition to which there is no behaviourist equivalent.

So we come at last to the probably unexpected conclusion that the superiority of the Hicksian method can be established on purely *operational* grounds alone!

And yet, when one comes to think of it, the result was not entirely unexpected. So long as the introspectionist method enables us to use, and the behaviourist method forces us to reject, a hypothesis which though not itself operational has operational consequences, we are bound to encounter the possibility that one such consequence can be predicted by the former method but not visualised by the latter. The case in which the income-elasticity of demand is nil, provides us with just such an instance where the operational consequence of a non-instantial proposition (the indifference hypothesis) is not mixed up with an operational proposition (such as the income-effect). It is, indeed, the *preparedness* for situations such as these which goes to establish the advantage of the method of introspection over simple behaviourism: in our instance, of the Hicksian indifference-preference theory over the revealed-preference theory of Samuelson.

IV

As would readily be seen, we regard the 'substitution effect' as a refutable inference from the generally non-instantial hypothesis of indifference. We have admitted that it is impossible to *measure* this effect except when the income-elasticity of demand is observed to be zero. But it is nevertheless possible to deduce its *existence* from empiric observations alone, as the following demonstration would show, even when the 'income effect' is observed to be positive.

Consider a case in which the consumer lives in a three-commodity world consisting of X, Y and Z. Suppose that his income is fixed and given in terms of Z, which therefore acts as the money in the system; and that the consumer buys quantities of X or Y by spending his Z on them. Let us suppose also that the consumer is observed to increase (decrease) his demand for X when his income alone rises (falls). Now what should we understand by the term, 'his income alone rises (or falls)'? Amongst other things the term would imply that the consumer's money income rises (or falls) but the prices of X and Y do not change. The income effect is therefore observed in isolation when real income changes, but prices remain constant. If, however, one of the prices change, real income will obviously have moved in the opposite direction of the price-change. If, for example, the price of X (alone) falls, the consumer's real income rises. Now, in the event of a given price-change, such as, say, a fall in the price of X, either the fact of the change in price will modify or offset (or prevent) the operation of the income effect (which is the supposed tendency of the consumer to buy more of a thing when he is better off, less when worse), or simply it will not. Let us assume first the latter to be the case.

If the price of X alone falls, assuming that the income effect remains unaffected, the consumer (finding himself better off than before) will buy more of X *and more of Y*. The price of Y remaining the same, he will therefore spend more on Y than he did before. He will, in consequence, have made a smaller outlay on X, his total income in terms of Z remaining fixed. His demand for X, therefore, will be observed to have a price-elasticity which is less than unity. Provided that neither X nor Y is an 'inferior' good, the assumption that income effect alone is present when the price of X (or of Y) alone changes, will therefore make the existence of both positive income-elasticity and a greater-than-unity price-elasticity of demand incompatible.

Thus the existence of 'elastic' demand leads us to abandon the hypothesis that the income effect alone can give a satisfactory account of the working of the demand theorem. When the price-elasticity of demand is observed to be greater than unity *and* the income effect (from the observation of the income-elasticity of demand) is known to be positive for all the commodities concerned, we can deduce that the given change in price has had an impact on demand over and above the simple income effect. When the price of X changes and the demand for it is found to be 'elastic', then something clearly must have happened which has reinforced the income effect on the consumer's demand for X while offsetting the income effect on his demand for Y. There has been, in other words, a *substitution effect* which reduces the outlay on Y when the price falls, increases it when the price of X rises. Given the income effect, the substitution effect is therefore residually defined and the two effects constitute together the full description of the operation of the demand theorem.

The demonstration of the operational meaningfulness of the substitution effect constitutes a further proof that the Samuelson-type demand theorem would have a smaller empiric content than the Hicks version. This interesting conclusion, as we have already observed above, appears paradoxical only at first sight, for results of this type were entirely to be expected from methodological considerations alone.

CHAPTER VIII

The Behaviourist Cardinalist

I

There is one tacit assumption underlying all three variants of utility theory reviewed in the preceding chapters: that any situation appearing to the individual as an alternative end is to be regarded as a 'sure prospect'. In other words, it is assumed that no element of uncertainty enters into the individual's prospect of reaching a stated end. Granting this simplifying assumption, as our previous analysis would suggest, we are more or less able to dispose of the cardinalist claims to absolute measurability of utility. Neither on grounds of expediency in formulating a general demand theorem nor from any other operationally relevant consideration is it necessary to admit the cardinalist hypothesis in utility theory.[1] Whether, as has frequently been claimed, we have to qualify or abandon this conclusion in the presence of uncertainty, is a question which must now occupy our attention.

It is easy enough to see that any type of utility theory must be futile in the presence of pure (complete) uncer-

[1] Though the usual 'Occam's razor' argument is quite sufficient to dispose of the orthodox cardinalist case as is implied here, we have already noticed that the failure of the cardinal theory to reconcile the demand theorem to the assumption of constant marginal utility of money provides a more positive ground for its rejection. See Chapter V, Section IV above.

tainty.[1] So long as uncertainty can be ruled out, it is axiomatic both in ordinalist and in cardinalist utility theory that a rational man necessarily prefers a larger amount of a given commodity to a smaller amount. Thus, for example, two units of a thing would always be preferred to only one unit of it. This is the basic axiom of rational choice without which it seems impossible to build up a workable utility theory. And it is this axiom which breaks down completely with the introduction of pure uncertainty: it can no longer be regarded as obviously rational, for example, that two birds (in the bush) should be preferred to one (in hand).

What is true of pure uncertainty is also true of *measurable risk* at least so far as the ordinalist theory is concerned. There can be no *ordinalist* ground for retaining the rationality axiom in the form, say, 'a more than 50 per cent chance of catching two birds in the bush is worth more than having one in hand.'

But it has been the contention of a large group of cardinalists in recent years, that measurable risk, far from presenting an obstacle in the way of measuring utility,

actually provides a method for an experimental verification of the cardinal utility hypothesis. This particular type of neo-cardinalist revival has drawn its inspiration largely from the work of Oskar Morgenstern and John von Neumann, though it is to Milton Friedman and L. J. Savage that the presentation of the operationalist case is

[1] We have used the term 'uncertainty' here in the sense of F. H. Knight (*Risk, Uncertainty and Profit*). Armstrong, however, uses it in quite a different sense, so that he can visualise 'uncertainty' as ordinally measurable. See, W. E. Armstrong, 'Uncertainty and the Utility Function', *Economic Journal*, March 1948.

mainly due.[1] The present chapter is devoted to an examination of the Morgenstern-Neumann type of utility theory in the context of situations involving measurable risk.[2]

II

It is necessary first of all to emphasise that the cardinalists following Morgenstern and von Neumann have an important thing in common with the ordinalists like Samuelson and Little: they share the same behaviourist methodology. Thus 'utility' is defined by the former, as by the latter, in terms of observed behaviour. But what distinguishes the cardinalist definition is that it is *statistical*, so that utility is inferred from a number of observations and not from a single act of choice.

We had observed in the last chapter that the principle of consistency presents a dilemma to the operationalist in utility theory: if he admits the procedure of drawing conclusions from the observation of single acts of choice he is forced to rule out the concept of 'indifference'; and if he wants to have the concept of 'indifference', he has to go without the economy of deriving conclusions from single

[1] The literature is extremely prolific, but the following may be mentioned as some of the path-breaking contributions: Friedman and Savage, 'Utility Analysis of Choices involving Risk', *Journal of Political Economy*, August 1948; Marschak, 'Rational Behaviour, Uncertain Prospects and Measurable Utility', *Econometrica*, 1950; Mosteller and Nogee, 'An Experimental Measurement of Utility', *Journal of Political Economy*, October 1951. The Morgenstern-von Neumann utility index was first proposed in their celebrated, *The Theory of Games and Economic Behaviour*.

[2] What follows is an experimentalist version of the cardinal utility index interpreted probabilistically. An algebraic and purely axiomatic version yielding a non-refutable index would be useless for our purpose. See Davis and Mellon, 'Majumdar on Behaviourist Cardinalism' and Majumdar, 'A Reply', *Economica*, August, 1960.

events. While Samuelson and Little have chosen the first
alternative, our neo-cardinalists have chosen the second.

It is possible to define preference in statistical terms both
in a 'strong' and a 'weak' sense: If the individual is observed *always* to choose a situation P, say, rather than a
situation I, regardless of the number of observations made,
P may be defined to be preferred to I, in a *strong* sense.
Thus we may consider a set of situations such as P, each
of which is 'strongly' preferred to I. Similarly if the individual is always found to choose I rather than a situation
R, we may say that I is 'strongly' preferred to R. And so we
may consider a set of situations such as R, any one of
which would always be rejected when compared to I.
Now, between the situations belonging to set P (in the
presence of which I is never chosen), and the situations belonging to set R (in the presence of which I is never rejected), may be conceived an intermediate set of situations
compared to any member of which the frequency of
choosing (or rejecting) I would lie somewhere *between*
zero and hundred per cent (but not quite the one or the
other). When a situation belonging to the intermediate
set is presented as an alternative to I, we can no longer predict the individual's choice for any *single* occasion. We
may then say that the individual is in a state of 'indifference' (which must be understood in a 'weak' sense here),
between I and any one member of that set. Or, alternatively, we may define any situation, say, P' to be *preferred*
to I in a *weak sense*, if over a number of situations the individual is found to be choosing P' rather than I more often
than not (but not always). Similarly we may have R' to
which I is preferred in a weak sense. Finally, we may have

I', which when presented as an alternative to I, is *chosen
as frequently* as I is. We may now define I' to be in a state of
statistical *strong* indifference with I. The statistical definitions of preference and indifference are illustrated on
the diagram below.

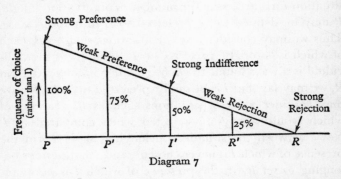

Diagram 7

Let us consider some of the immediate implications of
the statistical approach towards the definition of preference and indifference. In the first place, if the individual
is found to take, say, X rather than Y in one single instance
and Y rather than X in another, what shall we now make of
it? Evidently, we must first decide whether the statistical
evidence refers (*a*) simply to a change in the individual's
preferences or (*b*) to the absence of strong preference (and
therefore the presence of weak preference *or* indifference)
between X and Y. A moment's reflection would show that
no answer to this question can be offered which would
satisfy the behaviourist's criterion of 'meaningfulness'. No
amount of observation can either refute or establish the
hypothesis that the individual's preference pattern has
not itself undergone a change in course of our observation.

And surely, without some such hypothesis the description of observed frequency of choice as 'preference' or 'indifference' sounds at least unwarranted if not quite illegitimate. The behaviourist theory, therefore, cannot claim for itself (as it certainly does), the right of rationally predicting individual behaviour, without flouting its own rule of admissibility of hypotheses! However, this curious and incidental concession to the introspectionist (hypothetico-deductive) method, it must in fairness be admitted, manages to save 'positive' economics from complete barrenness.

Granting (however inconsistently) that it *is* possible to decide whether a change in relative preferences has (or rather, has not) taken place without having to introduce a fresh non-operational hypothesis, the statistical definitions of preference and indifference are still not completely free from ambiguity. Faced with two contradictory single instances (and *assuming* that preference has not changed), we still must decide whether the evidence refers to (*a*) a relation of only *weak* preference or (*b*) one of indifference. With only two observations to go upon, the question clearly must remain undecided. Even when there can be more than two observations we may interpret 'preference' and 'indifference' for our purpose only on the basis of a procedural resolution, because how many observations constitute the right sample to base our judgment upon must necessarily be somewhat arbitrarily decided. As we shall presently see, the problem of choosing the right size of the sample is inextricably connected with the more familiar question of two-term consistency.

The emergence of weak preference or statistical indifference at once raises the question: what happens now to the requirement of consistency? Obviously, it would no longer do to say that a person choosing X rather than Y in one single instance while choosing Y rather than X in another, is behaving inconsistently. But surely without an operationally meaningful definition of 'consistent' behaviour on the basis of which predictions can be made and tested the behaviourist theory loses its very content? It can be shown that the question 'What constitutes consistent behaviour?' cannot be answered in statistical terms except in the context of our question, 'What is the minimum size of the sample on which the preference (indifference) hypothesis can be based?' A simple example would perhaps be useful in illustrating the vital relationship between the two questions.

Suppose that an individual is observed to exercise his choice between two alternatives X and Y. Suppose also that the following observations of his choice are made: X is chosen in the first and the third instances; Y is chosen in the second, the fourth and the fifth. Clearly, on the basis of the first three observations X is found preferred to Y; but on the basis of the first four the relation between X and Y appears to be one of indifference, while on the basis of all five Y is found to be preferred to X.

Had we been invited to predict this individual's behaviour over a large number of cases from the first three, four and five observations respectively, what justification in each case should we have in making a forecast? Conceivably none, excepting the hypothesis that the said individual *would* behave on the whole consistently with his *so-far-revealed* preference. But what if the individual does *not* behave consistently with his so-far-revealed preference? Will the behaviourists pronounce him inconsistent? By no means: for he is now discovered to have been behaving perfectly consistently with his *now-revealed* preference! Thus so long as 'consistency' is defined *relatively* to the *totality* of observations made, its definition will remain necessarily circular. Unless, therefore, a somewhat arbitrary procedural restriction (determined empirically by sampling theory) is imposed upon the meaning of 'consistency', no man can be found inconsistent *ex post* though the best of forecasts goes wrong.

An obvious procedural restriction on the meaning of consistency which at once suggests itself can be stated in its most primitive form as follows: 'A given statistical choice is defined to be consistent (*a*) if it is observed to be the resultant choice in a sample S, when S is smaller than the total number of observations made; and (*b*) if it is also observed to be invariably the resultant choice for any other sample S', when S' is larger than or is as large as S. In other words, the same choice relation should have been observed not only for the total number of observations, but also for a smaller minimum number. This rather stringent restriction would imply that in the above illustration we are not at any stage provided with an evidence of consistency as now defined; and therefore, at no stage is predictability of the individual's behaviour indicated. It is only when a given statistical choice has been repeatedly observed in a set of samples of a minimum size, that some sort of consistency is established in a procedural (but not in the logical) sense, and a basis is found for the 'induction' of the behaviourist statistical-preference hypothesis.

We see, therefore, that the basic methodological dilemma in utility theory, which must remain unresolved on the logical plane, can now be stated as follows: suppose that we wish to formulate a utility hypothesis so that (a) it would include 'indifference', i.e., have weak ordering; (b) it would be based on strict two-term consistency, in the sense that if A (say) is preferred to B in any *one* situation, it is defined to be preferred to B for *all* situations; and (c) it would be defined strictly in terms of actually observed behaviour. It is obvious that while each is possibly a commendable end, we can only choose any two of '(a)', '(b)' and '(c)' as the foundations of our theory but *not* all three together. Thus '(a, b)' would give us the usual Hicksian hypothesis which would preclude '(c)' because 'indifference' cannot be defined as an observed single act of choice. '(b, c)' would be the method of Samuelson and Little which rules out 'indifference', i.e., '(a)'. Finally, as we have seen above, '(c, a)' gives us the statistical Morgenstern-Neumann type of theory which admits the concept of indifference but only by ruling out the requirement of single-events consistency, i.e., '(b)'.[1]

III

The assumption of a 'weak' *but* consistent preference (indifference) hypothesis is capable of rational explanation only on the basis of either (or both) of two possible assumptions. According to the first, the individual is taken to be quite unable to *discern confidently* between the two objects

[1] Incidentally, it may be pointed out that the recent Hicksian 'revision' of demand theory seems to be based on a curious misapprehension of this basic predicament in utility theory. See, *A Revision of Demand Theory*, Part I, 'Foundations', pp. 1–46.

concerned: he shows his preference (indifference) only with some hesitation. He may, therefore, be found to be occasionally choosing what eventually turns out to be the less desirable alternative. This assumption does not imply that the objects of choice before the individual are themselves uncertain; it is only that the distinction between these from the point of view of the individual's welfare is not clearly discernible to him.

According to the second assumption, weak preference would imply that the individual does not regard the two objects (or at least the better of the two) as 'sure prospects'. This would mean that the individual has to choose between a given probability of having (i.e., a certain risk of not having) one object and a different probability of having (i.e., a different risk of not having) another. The assumption would *not* imply that the individual could not discern confidently between two *sure* prospects, which would be the meaning of the first assumption.

We have argued in the following chapter how the first assumption (which has to be expressed mainly in introspective terms) leads logically to the Marginal-Preference theory of W. E. Armstrong thus providing the non-behaviourist account of the cardinalist revival. It is the second assumption which forms the basis of the behaviourist-cardinalist theory.

It must be made clear, however, that the rational 'explanation' of weak preference and statistical indifference forms no part of behaviourist theory as such. It is enough for the purpose of an operationalist to be able to hold that individuals behaved *as if* consistent weak preference existed. Similarly, it is possible to add a second 'explanatory' assumption in the next stage of the behaviourist argument which may help us understand *why* the individual should be expected to behave according to the behaviourist hypothesis, viz., that he invariably chooses that prospect of which the *statistically* expected value is the maximum. Needless to emphasise that the behaviourist argument is again satisfied *if* the individual is observed to behave so as to confirm the hypothesis. But since it should help *us* to place the behaviourist argument in its proper perspective, we must briefly note the nature of the possible 'explanation' behind the statistically-expected-utility-maximisation hypothesis.[1]

If the existence of risk provides the explanation of the phenomenon of 'weak' preference which implies that the frequency of choice is less than hundred per cent, it is not unreasonable to expect that other things remaining the same, the frequency of choice would vary (inversely) with the degree of risk involved. Or, in other words, given the degree of risk *and* other things, the frequency of choice should be invariant. Now, if we could add that given the degree of risk, the frequency of choice varies with the *intensity* of preference, then this frequency can certainly serve as a measure of relative preference under condition of risk.

But when we assume that under conditions of measurable risk the individual expresses his relative preferences in terms of the frequency of his choices, then we are also assuming something else; we can expect that the indivi-

---

[1] It is somewhat reassuring to note, however, that the plain behaviourist attitude to 'explanations' does not find favour with Marschak. See his, 'Rational Behaviour, Uncertain Prospects and Measurable Utility', *Econometrica*, 1950.

dual (to be rational) would be expressing his preferences statistically *only if* he knew or had reasons to believe that he would have to take the same choice-decisions an indefinitely large number of times. Given this assumption, however, no wonder that the consumer is expected to evaluate his 'prospects' in terms of statistical probability, and, judged over a large number of cases, to appear to maximise the statistically-expected value of his 'utility': which, precisely, is the neo-cardinalist-utility hypothesis. ⚲

IV

A cardinal-utility index is simply derived from the neo-cardinalist hypothesis thus: Suppose that the individual is faced with three alternatives, X, Y and Z. Suppose also that in the absence of risk, the individual is found to prefer X to Y; Y to Z; and therefore X to Z. Let us now consider a probability 'p' (say, $= \cdot 6$) in the prospect of getting X, associated with a probability of '$(1-p)$' of getting Z. Suppose that the individual is observed to prefer the prospect $X_{p=\cdot 6}$, $Z_{1-p=\cdot 4}$ to the certainty of getting Y. Let us now proceed to reduce the value of 'p' and so manipulate it as eventually to arrive at an appropriate value (say, $\cdot 5$) for which the individual is found to be indifferent between the prospect X, Z and the certainty of Y. Given our utility hypothesis, the individual evaluates his prospects statistically and equates:

$$p \cdot u(X) + (1-p) \cdot u'(Z) = u''(Y)$$

when $u(X)$, $u'(Z)$, $u''(Y)$ represent the utility levels associated with X, Z and Y respectively.

If we now fix our arbitrary origin at Z (the value of the

utility function at Z being $=0$), and so choose our scale as to have the value of the utility function at $Y=1$, we find

$$p \cdot u(X) = 1$$

Remembering that the relevant value for 'p' was $=\cdot 5$, we get the value of the utility function at X to be $=2$.

Thus our utility function is found to be measurable except for arbitrary origin and scale; it is measurable, in other words, up to a linear transformation. We have already seen that this implies a higher degree of measurability of utility than normally is assumed under ordinal theory.[1] The utility index worked out above can specify not only the signs of first differences (i.e., state the order of preferences) which is all that a purely ordinal index (measurable up to monotonic transformations) does, but also the signs of second differences (i.e., arrange *preferences* in order). If the individual is known to prefer A, B, C, D, etc. in that order and no other information is available, the implied utility index, as we may recall, is unique only up to a monotonic transformation. If it is also known, say, that the individual prefers A to B more (less) than he prefers B to C, etc., then the implied index is unique up to a linear transformation. While in the first case only A, B, C, etc. can be ordered, in the second we can also order the relative preferences of A over B; B over C; C over D, etc. But we *do not*, let it be emphasised, arrive at any additive quantities in the second case any more than in the first. What the second case permits us to measure is the *change* in welfare, and that measurement itself is ordinal.

---

[1] See Chapter III above.

See also, A. A. Alchian, 'The Meaning of Utility Measurement', *American Economic Review*, 1953.

If the *ordinal* measurability of a *change* in welfare (of marginal utility, if so defined) is all that the cardinalists have meant all along by a *cardinal* measurability of welfare (or utility), then the above index no doubt measures welfare or utility cardinally. But how many ordinalists would bother to deny that the sign(s) of the second differences can be known from an index obtained under 'ideal' conditions?[1] How many cardinalists would agree that this is all that their precious 'cardinalism' boils down to? True, that the Morgenstern-Neumann index is empirically more restrictive than a purely ordinal one, but that does not make it either (*a*) a quantitative index or even (*b*) an index which would be more generally useful.

The Morgenstern-Neumann index is supposed to be useful *only* under conditions of measurable risk. It does not seek to replace the ordinal-utility index under any other conditions. Therefore, even if it were valid and useful, its applicability would be limited. How severely indeed it would be, even under those 'ideal conditions' which are the operationalist's constant resort, it is necessary for us now to realise.

To have a situation in which the individual would ideally proceed in the neo-cardinalist manner in determining his choice, a number of assumptions regarding the *nature* of the object of choice are involved. Let us suppose that X is an 'ideal' object which is amenable to treatment by the Morgenstern-Neumann utility index: and let us now find out what X can (or cannot) possibly be.

In the first place, X must itself be measurable in quanti-

[1] Cf. for example, L. C. Robbins, 'Robertson on Utility and Scope,' *Economica*, May 1953.

tative terms. Therefore, X *cannot* be (*a*) an alternative '*social*' policy (preferring nationalisation to price-control; education to defence; Jones to Smith as cricket captain); or (*b*) an '*indivisible*' (though otherwise quantifiable) item (preferring *The Guardian* to *The Times*).

In the second place, we have to assume that decisions involving the choice of X are observed to be taken in large numbers, so that the chance of having X (i.e., the risk of missing it) can be calculated. The list of objects to be excluded from being X because of this assumption is likely to be so overwhelmingly large that we are almost tempted to invite the reader to include *any* '*real*' item of consumption in his black list!

In the third place, it is assumed that the 'risk', so calculated, is *known* to the individual. We need offer no comment on this rather convenient assumption except that it is not at least obviously plausible.

Finally, we make the crucial assumption that this knowledge of the statistical risk, somehow imparted to the consumer, is at all *relevant* information to him; which it would only be *if*, the consumer *himself* is expecting to take the decision of choosing or not choosing X a sufficiently large number of times. How many decisions, even under the ideal conditions, would satisfy this last requirement?

What then, can we finally surmise about the nature of 'X', the ideal neo-cardinalist consumer good? What could it conceivably be that was (*a*) itself quantifiable and divisible; (*b*) observed to have been chosen in sufficiently large numbers; (*c*) having its own 'risk-coefficient' attached to it as a tag for the consumer to see (*d*) also expected to be offered to the same individual a sufficiently large number of times so that the 'risk-coefficient' tag provided him with a genuine guide to rational behaviour?[1]

The object, we venture to say, which does satisfy more or less all the four assumptions and thereby reasonably qualify for being the ideal Morgenstern-Neumann 'X' almost suggests itself: it is a *simply calculable money-prize in a controlled game of chance.* Little wonder, therefore, that the celebrated Mosteller-Nogee 'experimental measurement' of the cardinal-utility index should happen to be a study of behaviour of men playing *suitably simplified* dice-and-poker games![2]

[1] It *is* rather baffling that these considerations do not weigh too heavily on the neo-cardinalist conscience. Is it not rather amusing that we should be tempted with the 'richer empiric content' of the cardinal-utility index? Cf. Friedman and Savage, 'The Expected Utility Hypothesis and the Measurability of Utility', *Journal of Political Economy*, 1952.

[2] 'An Experimental Measurement of Utility', *Journal of Political Economy*, 1951.

CHAPTER IX

The Introspective Cardinalist — A Revival

I

This chapter will be devoted to a consideration of the utility theory of W. E. Armstrong,[1] who, as our title would suggest, stands in the tradition of Alfred Marshall. The position of Armstrong in utility theory is, however, somewhat peculiar. Essentially an 'orthodox' cardinalist, he has forged his own tools to re-establish the orthodoxy. And it is his tools (which resembling those of some of his opponents a shade too closely, are subtly different) and not his conclusions, as we shall eventually find out, that has made this one-man school of thought an important variant of neo-cardinalism.

Armstrong's theory is based on two (for him) interdependent concepts: 'uncertainty', and 'indifference'. Terminologically, both are reminiscent of the behaviourist cardinalist, and the latter, also of the introspective ordinalist. We shall find, however, that both these terms are taken

[1] See, W. E. Armstrong, 'The Determinateness of the Utility Function', *Economic Journal*, 1939; Utility and the Theory of Welfare', *Oxford Economic Papers*, October 1951; Jerome Rothenberg, 'Marginal Preference and the Theory of Welfare', and W. E. Armstrong, 'A Reply', *Oxford Economic Papers*, October 1953; Jerome Rothenberg, 'Reconsideration of a Group Welfare Index: A Rejoinder on Marginal Preference', *Oxford Economic Papers*, June 1954; Tapas Majumdar, 'Armstrong and the Utility Measurement Controversy', *Oxford Economic Papers*, February 1957.

up by Armstrong to denote concepts to which neither the followers of Milton Friedman nor those of J. R. Hicks would normally be used.

Armstrong, too, would emphasise (like the behaviourist cardinalists) that the ordinal theory breaks down in the presence of uncertainty. But he would attach a slightly different meaning to his 'uncertainty' and a somewhat different analysis would therefore follow. As we had noticed in the last chapter, it is possible to have any one of two different assumptions which would go to explain uncertain (but rational) behaviour on the part of the consumer. One is that the objects of choice are found by the consumer to be uncertain *prospects*: though the *nature* of the end is certain, one is not sure how far the end would be achieved. This is the assumption on which the Morgenstern-Neumann cardinal-utility index is based. The other is that the consumer is not able to distinguish, from the point of view of his *welfare*, two otherwise certainly distinct ends. It is this second type of uncertainty: uncertainty in *discernment* of economic welfare and not uncertainty in the *prospect* of achieving a given economic end, which provides the basis of Armstrong's utility theory.

Armstrong also uses (like the Hicksian ordinalists) the concept of transitive preference. His 'indifference' is, however, unlike its Hicksian namesake, an *intransitive* relation, and is directly linked with his definition of 'uncertainty'. The consumer is supposed to be indifferent between two given ends, according to Armstrong, when he cannot perceive a distinction between the two. Since there may still remain a small (not quite perceptible) difference between two situations which the consumer just cannot distinguish, therefore this relation of indifference cannot be necessarily transitive. The consumer may not see the difference between, say, A and B, or between B and C, and yet (A proving to have been imperceptibly better than B, and B imperceptibly better than C), the difference between A and C may be just wide enough to be quite perceptible to him.

Had Armstrong been merely content with advancing his two propositions regarding the nature of consumer-uncertainty and the nature of indifference, the ordinalist would find in these very little to quarrel about. For neither Armstrong's concept of 'uncertainty',[1] nor his definition of 'indifference' has anything particularly *cardinalist* about it. It is the use to which these concepts have been put by Armstrong, as we shall see below, which is illegitimate from the ordinalist standpoint. It would be evident from our analysis of Armstrong's theory that instead of establishing cardinalism he has *assumed* it, but without ostentation: addibility of utility, both for the same person *and interpersonally* is implicitly axiomatic to him! Granted this contention about Armstrong's theory, our conclusion is, of course, obvious. While his new concepts lend considerable insight into the complexities of consumer-behaviour and can lead to definite modification of (ordinal) utility theory as we know it, these do not prove a thing for cardinalism of the orthodox school.

We have gone into some length in the following two sections over stating what we consider to be two rather important first principles: one concerning the definition of

[1] Cf. also, N. Georgescu-Roegen, 'Choice, Expectation and Measurability', *Quarterly Journal of Economics*, November 1954.

'indifference', and the other, the exact place of inter-personal comparisons in group-welfare economics. Our criticism of Armstrong's cardinal preference theory is based on what appears to us to be the obvious implication of these first principles.

II

Our first point is merely to contend that Armstrong's notion of 'indifference' and the usual ordinal notion are not necessarily incompatible. In fact, the two notions may indeed refer to two complementary propositions about the nature of consumer preference. It is our thesis that while the ordinalist idea is derived from the principle of *compensation*,[1] the Armstrong definition is derived from the idea of *approximation*. Whereas there is nothing wrong in supposing that in practice the compensation actually calculated to offset the consumer's loss may only be approximate, in theory it never need be so. Thus one can be indifferent between two states either (*a*) because in one the loss in any particular direction has been compensated for by a gain in another direction, or (*b*) because one state is perceived to be approximately the *same* as the other. While the first kind of indifference is clearly the result of the consumer's judgment of pros and cons, the second kind is the result of his inability (or unwillingness) to perceive small differences. It is not our contention, however, that the two kinds of indifference need always or ever be distinct in the consumer's actual state of mind.

We have already seen how the so-called indifference 'curves' in ordinal preference theory are derived through a

---

[1] Cf. Chapter VI, Section III above.

process of substitution. Armstrong's definition of 'indifference' follows, however, altogether a new line of thought. Indifference, he would argue, is only an imperceptibly low state of preference. To arrive at this interesting definition it is necessary to introduce the concept of an 'intensity' of preference, which can be high, low, or imperceptible as the case may be. This, Armstrong has been able to do very elegantly indeed as the following line of argument will show. What is even more remarkable is that Armstrong arrives at his own definition apparently from ordinal considerations alone! It is doubly important, therefore, that we examine his argument rather closely: if it stands, then the usual ordinal theory falls to the ground by the same principle of 'Occam's razor' by which it had been judged superior to orthodox cardinalism.

We can best explain Armstrong's point by a simple illustration. Let us suppose that an individual faces two possible welfare situations, A and D, and that for him ApD (using 'p' as the symbol for preference). If we now introduce a third possible situation C, and find that the individual prefers A to C and C to D, we may say that A, C, D can be arranged in a descending order of preference. Similarly we can have a fourth situation B, so that for the same individual: ApB, BpC, CpD; and so we may go on. Now the ordinalist, or so Armstrong would imply, is content merely with the statement that of the four welfare situations, the individual has a known relation of preference between any two, which fact can be read straight off the given preference scale. What the ordinalist was likely to overlook, however, Armstrong would allege, is that one can in fact read considerably more than that. Not only can one say, for example, that A is preferred to B, B to C and so on, one can surely add that the individual's preference for A over D, for example, must be *stronger* than his preference for A over B. In other words, there must always be rather more to choose between the very best and the worst, say, than between the best and the next best.

The above consideration at once introduces a new dimension in the description of ordinal preference: *preference-intensity*. The state of preference between situations A and D, can now be said to be more 'intense' than that between A and B. It is but one step from the admission of preference-intensity to the argument that as one goes on considering situations nearer and nearer to A in the individual's preference scale, his intensity of preference for A over each new situation will grow less and less. A point eventually will be reached when the individual is just barely able (or willing) to perceive the distinction between A and the new situation. The preference which the individual is *just* able to perceive, Armstrong defines as Marginal Preference. If A and A' are two situations so near to one another that the individual is barely able to see that he prefers A to A', then the two situations are separated, for that individual, by the natural unit of preference-intensity, Marginal Preference. If there is any situation P, nearer to A than is A', then the individual can no longer distinguish between the two situations A and P; he can no longer see the change in his welfare by moving from A to P or from P to A. The individual is then defined to be 'indifferent' between A and P. If P is a position between A and A', then similarly the individual would not be able to distinguish between P and A'. Thus, whereas he is indifferent between A and P and also between P and A', he is not indifferent between A and A'.

It is apparent that the term 'indifference' in Armstrong's definition stands for *approximate* identity of two situations. When an individual is said to be indifferent between A and P in the Armstrong sense, we can no longer say that his state of welfare remains the same in A as in P. All that we can say is that the difference between the two welfare levels, if it exists, is trivial. Armstrong's argument, therefore, does not raise any doubt as to the transitivity of the relation of 'equality'; it only questions the validity of overlooking the sum of a series of 'smalls', each one of which taken independently is negligible.

The existence of a state of indifference when the change in welfare is trivial is in no way incompatible with the existence of indifference due to a consideration that a given movement from one situation to another had included (at least in theory) full compensation. The relation of indifference due to the triviality of a difference will no doubt be intransitive. Such a relation will have a *hidden* direction (either positive or negative), and would tend at the limit to become a relation of simple preference. But this does not affect the proposition that indifference, based on compensation, will be transitive, i.e., it will show no tendency to add up to a relation of preference.

A diagram showing Hicks-Allen indifference *and* Armstrong indifference would not depict an indifference curve as a 'fuzzy' line. We should rather find, as in the diagram below, a sharply drawn line on which lie points representing situations linked in *transitive* indifference. Our line, however, would have an outlying shadow area. The indifference relation which would exist between any point in the shadow area and any point on the sharp line would be *intransitive*: i.e., there may not be existing a relation of indifference between any two points in the shadow. The network of indifference between *A, B, C, D and* each position in the shadow area taken separately, would be complete, while the network of indifference between positions in the shadow area may be non-existent or incomplete.

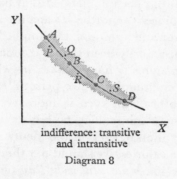

indifference: transitive
and intransitive

Diagram 8

III

In this section we shall deal with the problem of interpersonal comparison and the application of the Armstrong thesis to considerations of group-welfare. It is our contention, in the first place, that it is both possible and desirable to distinguish between the question of comparing individual welfares between persons and the question of aggregating individual welfares for a community of persons; and in the second place, that although Armstrong's cardinal preference theory supplies a partially satisfactory answer to the first question, it overlooks the second, and, therefore, takes us not much farther than a conventional theory of cardinal aggregation of welfare.

The problem of interpersonal comparison of welfare and the problem of aggregation of individual welfares are not identical. In fact, at least one of the common arguments usually put forward against the admissibility of welfare comparisons is really at bottom an argument against the admissibility of welfare aggregation. Whenever, to elaborate our point, it has been contended that one man's satisfaction or happiness cannot be set against another man's dissatisfaction or unhappiness, the implied logical difficulty has not necessarily been that of comparability. Even if we could imagine a happy state in which we were dealing with a community of two persons, each a spiritual replica of the other, and even if, moreover, we were endowed with some miraculous powers of measuring the welfare-consumption of each of the identical utility-twins in amounts like calories, we should not thereby be able to add up their welfares and *still make sense* of the total. The difficulty of so doing would lie in that so long as the twins are really two *different* persons, one man's happiness will not, *prima facie*, remove another man's suffering. The two would indeed cancel out in arithmetic: but the arithmetic would be meaningless in reality unless additivity of individual welfares is taken as *axiomatic*. The temptation of a neatly computed total showing aggregate group-welfare is no doubt great, but few would probably be happy to admit additivity explicitly, unless it could be demonstrated as tautologous with an intuitively more supportable axiom. On reflection it would appear that two such alternative axioms could possibly be offered, from either of which additivity could be derived, if necessary, as a theorem.

We may begin by stating the first possible alternative in these terms: 'The welfare of any individual in a given community will appear to be the welfare of each individual to each individual.' It follows that if one man were better off in consequence of a certain event, and another worse off, then for every individual in the community there would be a gain in welfare because of the former and a loss because of the latter. And what would emerge in the balance would be suffered or enjoyed by all. It would be as if the community in question reacted as an emotionally united family, where the joys and sorrows of every member were the joys and sorrows of all.

The above axiom, together with an additional one concerning the equality of men, constitutes the basis of what many people understand by democracy. Such utilitarian concepts as 'the greatest good of the greatest number', etc., would follow from the two axioms as logically valid theorems. Very often, however, this point is lost and the argument for the rule by the majority, for example, is interpreted as only an attempt at providing a sensible and tactful solution to a conflict of equals, which of course, in practice, democracy can often be.

We can replace what we may call the 'democratic' axiom of welfare-identity between persons as formulated above by another, which would conform to a rival system of ideals: 'Every individual is of account only as part of a whole, which is the community.' This axiom defined the community or the group as 'prior', in the sense perhaps of Aristotle, to the individual. It is the group, which is here the natural unit; it is only group life which is primarily meaningful. It must, however, be remarked that this axiom would not make the group independent of the individual. The group indeed is the sum; but the summing up is integration, not aggregation.

The above may well be described as the 'totalitarian' axiom of welfare-identity between persons. With or without a further axiom bearing on the equality of men, it would directly lead to propositions about the relationship between the state or the society and the individual, which are usually regarded as the fundamental opposites of the ideals of democracy

Whichever of the two axioms we might choose to admit, the transition from interpersonal comparison to community aggregation is rendered possible. Either the democratic or the totalitarian axiom would yield the following theorem of cardinal-welfare aggregation, *given*, of course, cardinal measurability of individual welfare: 'The increase in community-welfare due to an increase in one person's individual welfare is a full, more than full, or partial compensation for the decrease in community-welfare due to a decrease in another person's individual welfare.' Only on the validity of this theorem will depend the validity of any conclusion in cardinal terms regarding the welfare of a group of more than one person. The theorem seeks to provide a cardinalist solution to the summing up problem in group-welfare economics. As an index of change in the aggregate welfare of the community, it is indeed the cardinal opposite number of the well-known 'Pareto-criterion' in the ordinal analysis.

From what we had been saying above two things seem to

emerge in the main. First, the very well-known proposition that aggregation of welfare in a cardinal sense is impossible without ascribing *cardinal, comparable* properties to individual welfares; *and* second, that aggregation of welfare, in any case, would hardly make much sense unless it were presumed that the aggregate in arithmetic was also a meaningful category on the real plane. While it would be perfectly legitimate to appeal to results obtained through laboratory experiments and introspection to judge the nature of the welfare experience of the individual, the truth or otherwise of the principle of additivity is obviously neither demonstrable nor refutable. Unless, therefore, we are prepared explicitly to admit additivity through the introduction of one or other of the alternative axioms of welfare-identity between persons, even a demonstration of cardinality and comparability of individual welfare will not go very far in solving the summing up problem.

Turning now to Armstrong's interesting conclusions for group-welfare drawn from his cardinal-preference theory, we must, therefore, try to determine how far he has found it possible to meet the *two* essential questions we have discussed above: the question of comparison, and the more comprehensive question of aggregation.

Armstrong's main conclusions are very neatly brought out in a two-person model which has been the subject of some interesting controversy.[1] It would be useful at this stage to set down his model in the first place and then to proceed to an examination of his thesis in the light of what we have said in the earlier sections of the present chapter.

[1] Cf. the controversy between Armstrong and Rothenberg in the *Oxford Economic Papers*, loc. cit.

Let us consider a community of two persons (following Armstrong), say, X and Y. Suppose that X prefers a situation A to a situation B, while Y prefers B to A. Clearly, in purely ordinal terms, no group-preference between the situations A and B can emerge. Nevertheless, it is possible to construct a group-preference even in this case, or so Armstrong would contend, if the *intensity* of X's preference for A over B is known to be stronger (weaker) than the intensity of Y's preference for B over A. Obviously, if the two intensities were assumed to be comparable *and* addible *explicitly*, the resultant in terms of group-preference would at once follow. But Armstrong seems, at first sight, to be able to arrive at his interesting solution on the basis of only ordinal assumptions. We visualise (to follow his argument) for the individual X a situation C, so that he prefers A to C and also C to B. Similarly for Y, let us say that there exists a situation D, so that he is indifferent between B and D, and also between D and A. (Since the Armstrong type of indifference is not transitive this is quite consistent with Y still preferring B to A). Let us now offer individual X the situation C while at the same time offering Y the situation D. Let us call our composite offer (C to X, D to Y), O. We shall assume also that the C-for-X part of our offer has no effect on Y, and the D-for-Y part of it has no effect on X. Now evidently, if X has to choose between B and our offer he will take it; if he has to choose between A and our offer, he will reject it. Y will find that the difference in his welfare as between B and O, or again between O and A, is trivial; he will, therefore, be indifferent between B and O and between O and A. Therefore, if the situation A and the composite offer O is presented before the two-person group, X would prefer A to O and Y would not be worse off at A than at O. Applying the well-known Pareto criterion, the group as a whole therefore prefers A to O. Similarly if now O and B are presented before the group, X would find that his welfare is greater at O than at B, while Y would not be any worse off in either case. Therefore, again the group is found to prefer O to B. Since the group prefers A to O and O to B, and since preference is always transitive, the group prefers A to B.

Thus, surprisingly enough, we arrive at a determinate solution of the two-person problem by employing arguments which have at least superficially an ordinalist form. At first sight it does seem as though a clever but legitimate handling of the axiom of transitivity of preference and the ordinalist Pareto criterion were all that was needed to produce the rather paradoxical result of the Armstrong model. Our object is to demonstrate that it is not so, and that Armstrong obtained the determinate solution in his model by making an unwarranted extension in the meaning of transitivity of group-preference. But when we contend that Armstrong cannot arrive at his solution from ordinal considerations alone, we do so only to emphasise that Armstrong could not escape the twin question of comparability and additivity in his model.

A judgment on the curious method of deriving cardinal conclusions from ordinalist-looking argument as employed by Armstrong would rest on three main considerations: first, the permissibility of the definition of Marginal Preference, and consequently of intra-marginal indifference; secondly, the meaningfulness of the crucial composite offer of the situation O; and finally, the validity of assuming transitivity of group-preference for situations containing intransitive indifference relations.

So far as the definitions of Marginal Preference and intransitive indifference are concerned, we may only repeat what we have taken some pains to establish above: that there is no logical difficulty in defining preference-intensity[1] from purely ordinal considerations, nor any of visualising a minimum level of preference-intensity on the threshold of effective perception by each individual. So long as this minimum level of perception is left to itself, no cardinal (additive) meaning attaches to the concept of Marginal Preference, and the existence of approximate and intransitive indifference relations remains compatible with the existence of compensatory and transitive indifference relations. It is only when we start talking in terms of 'multiples' of the minimum level of perception that we assume additive cardinality and constancy as attributes of this level. So far as the explicit steps taken in the Armstrong illustrations are concerned, we may notice that the use of this latter cardinal extension of the idea of marginal preference has been carefully avoided. But the end-result of the two-person problem, as we shall argue, is unobtainable without this extension.

Coming now to the meaningfulness of the composite offer O, we are inclined to agree with Jerome Rothenberg that it does imply an impossible abstraction. Nevertheless, we do not think that Armstrong's argument really suffers much on this account. It is hardly plausible, it is true, that

[1] Note that this is exactly the same as assuming measurability of utility up to a linear transformation.

we should ever *find* a situation such as O, meaning one thing to X, and quite a different thing to Y. But, as we have ourselves tried to do above, it may quite easily be possible to visualise *two* situations at the same time: only C for X and only D for Y, and to assume additionally that possible disturbances in the preference patterns of X and Y due to external relations do not exist — an abstraction which ordinal theory also does not avoid. Thus the so-called composite situation (we have called it the composite 'offer') may quite legitimately serve as a useful point of reference without itself entering into the realm of observable reality, provided only that all consequences of external economies are ruled out.

The real snag in Armstrong's argument, in our opinion, becomes obvious only when we consider the question of transitivity of group-preference. At first sight it may appear that group-preference would be transitive provided only that individual preferences are. This, however, is by no means the case. When we say that the situation A is group-preferred to the situation O, we mean thereby that for every member of the group under consideration, the relation between A and O is *either ApO* (using 'p' as the symbol for preference as before), *or* one of indifference; and that for *at least one* member of the group the relation *is* ApO. In other words, at least one person must be better off and none worse off to enable us to say that the group as a whole is better off at A than at O (the Pareto criterion). Now it is only when group-preference is constructed strictly on the basis of a combination of *transitive* preferences and *transitive* indifferences that we require no additional postulate to argue its own transitivity. Thus if A is group-preferred to O, and similarly O to B, A can be said to have been group-preferred to B, *provided* that all those who are indifferent between A and O and also between O and B are indifferent between A and B. Surely the possibility that some people could always be led up the garden path, and moved without any resistance from A to O, O to B and so on, while they disapprove of being shifted from A to B directly, may have political advantages, but that would hardly be a relevant consideration in a theory of welfare. Obviously a progressive deterioration in the position of an individual (by way of systematic expropriation, for example), cannot be logically supported simply on the ground that it is a gentle and painless process, and at no stage of it does the individual perceive that he is slightly worse off than he was at the immediately preceding stage! Thus in postulating transitivity of group-preference Armstrong transgresses his own principle of intransitivity of indifference, and on this point alone the entire pseudo-ordinal structure of the argument in his model breaks down. What remains of it is only the concept of approximation in welfare perception, leading to the idea of marginal preference and intransitive indifference. To arrive at group-preference from these two relations we have to bring out all over again the question of comparability of individual welfares and the question of additivity of comparable individual welfares.

It may be remembered that we had ventured the opinion towards the beginning of this chapter that Armstrong has been able to provide only a partially satisfactory answer to the first question but none at all to the second. Marginal preference, Armstrong has argued, is the *same* for every individual and therefore, by definition the question of comparability does not arise. In spite of Rothenberg's objections, we are inclined to agree with the first part of this contention but not with the last. A change in welfare has been defined by Armstrong, as by most other people, in terms of the individual's *experience* of a change in the objective situation. Now for every individual, Armstrong contends, there should be a certain *minimum* level of change in the objective situation which *just* enables him to undergo the experience of a change in welfare. The minimum would no doubt be different for different persons or even for the same person at different times. But however different the *objects* of perception may be, these would induce the same *act* of perception, viz., the experience of the smallest perceivable difference in welfare. Thus Armstrong's 'unit' of welfare, Marginal Preference, is defined as the barest perception of a changed situation, and obviously, whatever the required change may be, marginal preference would be the *same experience*, by definition. Therefore the obvious possibility that one person may not be able to distinguish between two situations while another may find a hundred intermediate and easily demarked states between these two, is entirely irrelevant to the argument. In other words, the statement that X marginally prefers A to A' implies the same welfare difference as the statement that Y marginally prefers A to B or C to D. Thus comparability of individual welfares presents no problem on the threshold of welfare experience. The act of *bare* discernment of welfare by anybody has the same meaning.

In so far as Armstrong has drawn attention to the irrelevance of the comparison problem at the threshold of welfare experience, he has been able to take an important step towards the solution of the question of interpersonal comparability. It is possible that psychological experimentation would at some date be judged competent to prove or refute Armstrong's assumption that marginal preferences can be added arithmetically in the individual's experience, thereby providing a basis for the comparison of welfare perceptions which are wider than those at the threshold.[1] All that, however, will not help in settling the remaining and still intractable question of addibility of individual welfares and a meaningful cardinal derivation of group-preference given individual (ordinally *or* cardinally stated) preferences.

[1] Note that the possible solution of the problem of interpersonal comparability or that of the question of addibility of individual welfare at the psychological (or other non-economic) level would be irrelevant to economics. So long as the questions involved cannot be solved at the level of economic operation, the psychological, philosophical, etc. answers, however valid, would be 'meaningless' on the economic plane.

CHAPTER X

Some Concluding Remarks on Measurability of Utility

I

What, on balance, seems to have emerged out of the preceding pages on the Measurability question now deserves a final summing up. We offer below our concluding observations on the utility controversy in the following order: (*a*) a comment on the meaning of utility; (*b*) a comment on the meaning of cardinal measurability; and finally, (*c*) a comment on the choice between the strong-ordering and the weak-ordering hypotheses in ordinal-utility theory.

II

Utility or economic welfare is meaningful primarily only to the individual.[1] While the individual may (or may not) be able to perceive utility absolutely,[2] he cannot, in any case, describe his perception in an operationally useful sense without making a comparative statement about his alternatives.[3] Value judgments which are not comparative are useless data in economics. Therefore, whatever be the nature or the exact basis (physical, psychological, etc.) of his utility perception, the act of perception is useful (and

---

[1] See Chapter II, pp. 17–18.
[2] See Chapter III, pp. 33–34.
[3] See Chapter II, pp. 21–22.

so, relevant) information only as (or through) an act o comparison. Also, controversies regarding the nature o the basis of utility perception (on psychological, philosophical, etc. planes) are irrelevant to the question o measurability of utility as defined in terms of comparison of alternatives. Similarly, had utility been defined otherwise than in the sense of comparison between ends, the question of its measurability would have been irrelevant to welfare economics, but perhaps relevant to some other discipline.[1]

While the behaviourist *defines* an act of comparison as an act of choice (and rejection), the introspectionist suggests that an act of comparison (of the type: A would be better than B; C would compensate for the loss of B) is *behind* an act of choice (or perhaps, a demand for compensation). But in any case, the perception of utility, for the purpose of economics, *is* comparison between ends.[2]

Measurability of utility at least up to all monotonic transformations (simply involving statements such as 'A is preferred to B; B to C, etc.') is, therefore, essential to the *definition* of utility in economics: it is *not* part of an additional hypothesis. It is, consequently somewhat trivial to pose the cardinal hypothesis as an *alternative* to the ordinalist position. Cardinalism requires one extra hypothesis; ordinalism, strictly speaking, needs only the operational definition of utility.[3]

----

[1] Graaff seems to us to have been too hasty in dismissing the relevance of the measurability question. He is obviously arguing from some other (non-economic) definition of utility. See Jan de V. Graaff, *Theoretical Welfare Economics*, Cambridge, pp. 35–40.

[2] See Chapter II, pp. 22–23.

[3] See Chapter II, p. 23.

The question of measurability in welfare theory therefore implies the question whether statements such as 'A is preferred to B; B to C, etc.' can (need) be more precise and therefore more restrictive (i.e., no longer permitting all monotone transformations of a given utility function to describe it correctly) at least in principle.

III

How far does one have to go, beyond ascribing simple ordinal measurability (up to a monotonic transformation) to utility in order to be classed as a good cardinalist? We have seen that there is unlikely to be a semantic agreement amongst the cardinalists on this vital question. We have been able to specify at least two different meanings in which the term 'cardinalism' has been used in the literature of utility theory implying two different degrees of restriction (precision) to be assumed in the measurement of utility.[1]

The more obvious sense in which 'cardinalism' is used makes it almost identical with some form or other of an 'addible-utility hypothesis'. Thus, if somebody is known to be able to enjoy, say, 10 units of satisfaction from a situation A, and 5 units from a situation B, then he would enjoy, according to this hypothesis, 15 units of satisfaction when given both A and B.

We have seen that the cardinalist hypothesis, given this 'addibility-content', is not only (a) unnecessary, but also (b) liable to yield contradictory or false results in demand theory.[2] The Marshall-Robertson hypothesis has therefore been rejected by us without any qualification.

[1] See Chapter III, Section III.
[2] See Chapters V–VI.

The other sense in which the term 'cardinal' has been used implies only measurability up to a linear transformation.[1] Utility, according to this hypothesis, is like temperature, measurable except for the arbitrary origin and scale. That this does not imply addibility is obvious:[3] all that i implies is *ordinal* measurability of relative preferences (o the type: *A* is preferred to *B* more than *B* is preferred to *C* etc.).

It has been our conclusion that there can be no objection to ordinal measurability of relative preference (call it marginal utility) at the level of *introspection*. In fact, the idea that we sometimes consider the difference between the first (in order of preference) and the second to be somewhat less (more) important than the difference between the second and the third (say), does not appear to us to be disputable at all.[4]

What *is* disputable, however, is the idea that preference-intensity can be expressed at the level of *observation*. Suppose that one prefers *A* to *B* much more strongly than he prefers *B* to *C*. Can this have any operational consequence apart from those which would have followed even if one preferred *A* to *B* much *less* than *B* to *C*? The answer must be obviously in the negative unless we are prepared to ad-

[1] See Chapter VIII.

[2] This neo-cardinalist hypothesis would perhaps remind the reader of the original Benthamite 'felicific thermometer'. Cf. J. Viner, 'Bentham and J. S. Mill: The Utilitarian Background', *American Economic Review*, March 1949.

[3] This can be demonstrated at once. Suppose that we are comparing three degrees of temperature, *A*, *B* and *C*. These are, say, 212° F., 200° F. and 32° F. respectively. If these temperatures are addible, then clearly *B* and *C* together would be greater than *A*. But measure *A*, *B*, *C* in centigrades, and *B* plus *C* can never be greater than *A* (since *C* is 0° C.)!

[4] Cf. L. Robbins, 'Robertson on Utility and Scope', *Economica*, May 1953, p. 104.

nit the hypothesis of statistical consumer behaviour. We have tried to demonstrate the inadmissibility of this last hypothesis except perhaps in the context of a controlled game of chance.[1]

Cardinalism in the 'additive' sense is therefore found quite untenable; while in the 'measurable-up-to-linear-transformation' sense it is found completely inconsequential, except in an extreme situation, which is demonstrably unreal.

IV

On the dispute between the weak-ordering hypothesis of Hicks and the strong-ordering hypothesis of Samuelson, we shall have one final observation to make. It is simply that the dispute has served to bring out clearly a fundamental dilemma in utility theory. If we are prepared to admit the level of introspection into our theory, then the act of comparison may constitute indifference just as well as preference. If we are not, then no *single* act of choice can translate indifference into behaviour. Either, we choose to be completely operationalist and so dismiss the idea of indifference (and have the strong-ordering hypothesis) or, we agree to admit the non-observable level of introspection and have weak ordering.

Two apparently plausible solutions can be advanced to meet the Samuelsonian objection to the admissibility of weak ordering. It is our contention that both are false solutions.

The first attempt is due to Hicks.[2] He assumes that the

[1] See Chapter VIII.
[2] *A Revision of Demand Theory*, p. 41.

inadmissibility of weak ordering in a Samuelson-type theory arises from the consideration of the empirical fact that most goods are indivisible. Thus it is rather meaningless, one would say, to hold that the consumer is indifferent between 8 units of X, for example, and 7 units of X plus ·7 unit of Y, if ·7 unit of Y has no real existence. This objection can be met, Hicks points out, at least in the case of money, which is finely divisible. Given divisibility, he argues, the objection to the use of 'indifference' breaks down.

We have tried to emphasise that the basic behaviourist objection to 'indifference' has nothing whatsoever to do with the empiric objection due to indivisibilities. Even if all things were infinitely divisible, no single choice-event could express indifference. The real objection, as we have pointed out, is determined by methodology and not by facts.

We could suggest a second possible way of trying to overcome the methodological impossibility of combining 'indifference' with 'single-event consistency': While it is true, it may be argued, that the consumer cannot express his indifference in a single act of choice, we can nevertheless choose to include his 'statements' (such as, say, a demand for compensation) as observable events. This would apparently permit us to introduce the concept of indifference on behaviourist grounds alone!

The logical objection to our proposed solution is as follows. We cannot mix up a man's actual choice and his statement about his preference and put them both under the same category: for the latter is only *about* what the former is. To take them together is to open the door to fresh paradoxes. So long as the 'behaviour' of actual choice and the 'behaviour' of making statements about it differ in logical hierarchy, the one can run counter to the other without *logical* inconsistency. It is easy to see how consumer behaviour at the level of making actual choices and consumer behaviour at the level of making statements have no logically necessary operational consequences on one another. If, for example, the given individual is found to choose A rather than B, while he says that (i) he prefers A to B or (ii) he is indifferent between A and B, there will remain the same operational consequence of either '(i)' or '(ii)', viz., that he is found to choose A rather than B. Similarly, if the individual *says* that he is indifferent between A and B while he actually chooses (i) A rather than B or (ii) B rather than A, there will remain the one and the same operational significance of either '(i)' or '(ii)', viz., that he *says* that he is indifferent between A and B. Thus while one can easily have a behaviourist theory of consumer choice or a behaviourist theory of consumer 'protestations', one cannot have a behaviourist theory of consumer choice-cum-'protestations'!

But to say that one cannot have (a) weak ordering; (b) single-event-consistency; and (c) behaviourism all at the same time is *not* to say that there can be nothing to choose between the Hicksian $(a + b)$, the Samuelsonian $(b + c)$, and the statistical $(c + a)$ methods in utility theory. On the contrary, it has been our principal thesis that the ability to introduce non-instantial explanatory hypotheses (such as the Hicksian 'indifference') has an advantage over pure behaviourism *even in the enunciation of fully operational (testable) theorems*. In fact, to say that you cannot have everything is to say that you have to make your choice. In so far as we have succeeded in proving a number of 'impossibility theorems' *and* indicating our resultant choices, we have behaved as methodologist and economist together. For the methodologist is to the economist what the economist is to the rest of us.

APPENDIX

Choice and Revealed Preference[1]

I

One fundamental axiom in the behaviourist ordinal utility theory is that choice reveals preference. It is the purpose of this note to demonstrate that this axiom is invalid for situations where the individual choosers are known to be capable of employing strategies of a game-theory type. Such strategies are, of course, not needed in the perfect competition model usually assumed in discussions of ordinal tastes and observable preference.

To apply game theory of the usual type, one must have a cardinal utility or pay-off; given only ordinal utility, the usual game theory is limited in its applicability. Nevertheless, as the following rather paradoxical voting situation shows, there are cases where from ordinal utility considerations alone we can apply the 'saddle point' reasoning of the game theory more or less satisfactorily. As will be seen from this example, we economists must, in inferring from actual choice just what the underlying preference pattern truly is, take care: we must first be sure of the

[1] The present note appeared in substantially the same form in *Econometrica*, January 1956.

The author expresses his indebtedness to Professor B. Datta of the Presidency College, Calcutta, and to Professor P. A. Samuelson of the Massachusetts Institute of Technology, Cambridge, Mass., for many valuable comments on an earlier draft. All responsibility for what appears below is, of course, the author's own.

choices, that the observed individual feels, are open to him and must make hypotheses about the strategies that he may find it necessary to follow. Whenever in fact, a committee member (or a political party) considers the problem of finding a policy (or a candidate) that would combine optimally a fair measure of the sponsor's approval and a reasonably high chance of acceptance by the voting majority, the saddle point of decision is sought and often discovered.

II

Let us consider a very simple case involving a community of seven choosers (voters) among whom are two sponsors (two political parties or two combative members of a committee who habitually move all the resolutions). The sponsors set up candidates (or alternative policies) on which the choosers cast their votes. Let us call the sponsors F and G, and the other choosers A, B, C, D and E. Let the ordered preferences of the choosers facing alternatives (say) M, N, O and P be expressed as follows, the direction of preference being to the left:[1]

A:	N,	O,	P,	M;	E:	M,	O,	N,	P;
B:	P,	M,	O,	N;	F:	M,	N,	O,	P;
C:	P,	N,	M,	O;	G:	P,	O,	N,	M.
D:	O,	N,	P,	M;					

It is easily seen that in a vote, whichever of the two sponsors puts up his candidate first, loses. For example, if F sets up M for the community's approval, G can set up P

---

[1] The actual subjects of choice are quite immaterial for the present purpose: these could be as particular as alternative regulations for a football club, for example, or as general as alternative social states covering the whole life of a community.

and win by 5 votes to 2. If F sets up N, G can set up O and win by 4 votes to 3.[1] If, however, G is tempted to set up P first, F can sponsor N to win by 4 votes to 3; whereas if G sets up O first, F can now support M and win by the same margin.

Moreover, if we consider the problem of the sponsor F, then clearly, if he is forced to speak first, (a) sponsoring his *best* preference (M) will win the game for his worst (P); but (b) sponsoring his second preference N, will result in the victory for O, which would be better than his position in '(a)'. This shows that if F has to start the game, he will be ill advised to reveal his preference of M over N.[2]

It follows, therefore, (a) that the use of strategy will make it imperative for 'sponsor-choosers' (i) to bargain continually for the position of the last bidder; and (ii) sometimes to abandon or *reverse* a part of their actual preferences in a defensive bid to attain the position of the 'maximum minimorum';[3] and (b) that this last position

[1] Note that had G persisted in setting up P, his first preference, he would have lost by 3 votes to 4.

[2] Note that there is no such problem for sponsor G. If he has to speak first, his third preference will win when he puts up his first, and his fourth preference will win when he puts up his second.

[3] D. Black and K. Arrow have both noticed the curious situations where misrepresentation might help, as in the following case (cf. Kenneth J. Arrow, *Social Choice and Individual Values*, John Wiley & Sons, Inc., New York, p. 80, footnote 8):

A committee considers successive motions on a knockout principle, the winner of the first two being set against the third and so on. Let individual 1 have preferences X, Y, Z; individual 2, Y, X, Z; and individual 3, Z, Y, X. Suppose that the motions come up in the order Y, Z, X. If all individuals voted according to their orderings, Y would be chosen over Z and then over X. However, individual 1 could vote for Z the first time, and when Z wins as a result, in the second round the victory of X, his first preference, is assured, everybody voting according to his ordering.

The essence of game theory, however, hardly lies in these 'first order'

could be defined meaningfully in terms of ordinal preferences as that of the 'highest among the lowest', which, as an object of pursuit, could have an equal operational significance.

In the course of constructing the greatly simplified model of our illustration, we have made a number of implicit assumptions. Each of these, as one can readily see, places a constraint on the scope of strategy, rather than providing a special case for its employment in the exercise of choice.

Of the three major assumptions, the first relates to the sponsors' complete knowledge of the preference scales of the choosers. If this knowledge is incomplete, then that would only increase the number of possible 'guesses' by the sponsors (which is reduced to one in our illustration), and call for a more elaborate and flexible (though certainly less confident) use of stratagems. The second assumption is that more sponsors do not appear during the exercise of choice. But in case there *is* a third sponsor, that would only further complicate the strategy of each, the nature of the problem remaining unchanged. The third assumption, which incidentally has been made rather deliberately, is that the two sponsors do *not* try to change the preference scales of the choosers. In a truly dynamic situation, however, this is precisely what the sponsors must be expected to do. But we have distinguished the strategy involved in *changing* the preference patterns from the strategy involved in *using* the preference patterns, and

camouflages which assume that only one person can hide his hand (as in the Black case cited above); a game really involves *at least* 'second order' camouflages which forestall the strategy, the moves *and* the counter-moves of the opponent (as in our illustration).

have ruled out the former only to demonstrate how important a part stratagems can play even in a fairly static model.

All this leads us to conclude that in the presence of forestalling, choice need not reveal preference. The distortion of preference in observed choice, however, will not be haphazard: it would follow the defensive norm of the 'maximum minimorum' which can be made meaningful even when preferences are only ordinally expressed. An obvious implication of this is, of course, that the axiom that choice reveals preference has to be restated in the form: choice is derived from preference, in a manner so as to give the fullest weight to preference *eventually*; and this requires that preference be sometimes revealed in *immediate* choice, sometimes distorted or abandoned.

PRINTED IN GREAT BRITAIN
BY ROBERT MACLEHOSE AND CO. LTD
THE UNIVERSITY PRESS, GLASGOW